First steps in librarianship

A Students' Guide

K. C. Harrison

City Librarian of Westminster

Fourth Edition

COMPLETELY RE-WRITTEN

 ANDRE DEUTSCH / A Grafton Book

First published 1950 by
André Deutsch Limited
105 Great Russell Street London WC1

Reprinted 1950
Second edition 1960
Reprinted 1960, 1962
Third edition 1964
Reprinted 1964
Fourth edition 1973

Printed in Great Britain by
Ebenezer Baylis and Son Ltd
The Trinity Press, Worcester, and London

ISBN 0 233 96427 4

Contents

Preface to fourth edition

This fourth edition of *First steps in librarianship* has been requested by the publishers for some time now. It would have been prepared before this but for pressure of work. In some ways, however, the delay between the third edition and this one may prove to be advantageous to readers, because the science of librarianship, never static, has been moving quickly in the last few years, and I have been able to reflect the most important of these developments in this edition.

Since the third edition appeared, some of the developments I foreshadowed have come to full achievement. New legislation for public libraries in England and Wales has been put on the statute book and has already had much influence. Many new library buildings are functioning. Rapid developments have taken place in the field of library automation and data processing; international aspects of librarianship have grown apace; and, most important of all from the student's viewpoint, education for librarianship has undergone revolutionary changes not only in Britain but in many other countries as well.

I must repeat what I said in the preface to the third edition by reiterating that while it is true that advanced knowledge of some of these developments is not necessarily the province of the beginner, the author has had to revise the book against this backcloth of radical change, and has tried to take into consideration most of the significant developments.

This book began as an examination guide but it has gradually evolved away from that, and this fourth edition is not geared to any examination requirement. Instead it now offers itself as an introductory handbook to library science, suitable to be put into the hands of all professional newcomers, in whatever type of library they may be, and in whatever part of the world they may be.

For although the main concentration may still be upon

British practice, the attempt has been made to include a more cosmopolitan approach, and references to overseas library development and practice will be found to be more generous than they were in previous editions. Obviously, such references still have to remain brief in a handbook of these dimensions, but they are included in order to impress student librarians from the outset that librarianship is a truly international science, and that all countries have much to learn from each other's experience and progress.

Once again I express my debt to other textbooks and to the publications of the Library Association. I am also grateful to many colleagues, too numerous to mention, who have made useful comments on previous editions. The responsibility for opinions expressed remains, of course, entirely my own.

London, N20   K. C. HARRISON

Chapter 1
National, university and special libraries

There is a natural tendency on the part of the aspirant
librarian, young in experience, to assume that all libraries have
the same aims, methods and organization as the one in which
he is working. But it cannot be said early enough that there
exist many different types of libraries.

A brief list of these different types ought to indicate to the
beginner how varied they are in their objectives and consequent
administration. There are national libraries, university, college
and other academic libraries, public libraries, school libraries,
hospital libraries, newspaper libraries and medical libraries.
There are also the libraries of government departments, as well
as the libraries and information bureaux which are now common to large industrial firms, research associations, and many
professional societies and learned bodies. It should be appreciated that, although public libraries are in most countries the
largest employers of personnel, the number of non-public
libraries in the world greatly exceeds that of public libraries.

It is a common fault with beginners in the library field to
regard their own libraries and practices as being typical of all
others. While there are many basic techniques common to all
types of library, student librarians should appreciate, from the
outset, that in many details university library practice and
problems differ considerably from those of public libraries, and
that special library practice is entirely different from that
required in national libraries.

After these few introductory remarks, which it is hoped will
be borne in mind throughout the reader's studies and professional life, this chapter goes on to describe very briefly the
national, academic and special library fields, leaving public
libraries to be dealt with in the ensuing chapter.

NATIONAL LIBRARIES

Nearly every country in the world now has a national library, and it has been an encouraging sign to note how quickly the new independent countries have begun to build up essential national collections of books and related materials. Of course, the largest national libraries naturally belong to the older countries, and the world's biggest are undoubtedly the Library of Congress in Washington, D.C., the Lenin State Library in Moscow, and the British Museum Library in London.

These vast organizations not only possess large and rapidly increasing stocks, but are also extremely active in such projects as cataloguing and classification, and in the production of bibliographical material. But the smaller national libraries are not to be ignored. There are national libraries for Scotland in Edinburgh, for Wales in Aberystwyth, and for Ireland in Dublin, all of which are of signal importance. Among other great national libraries are the Royal Library in The Hague, the Royal Library in Brussels, the Royal Libraries in Copenhagen, Stockholm and Oslo, the Bibliothèque Nationale in Paris, and the National Library of Australia in Canberra, to mention only a few.

National libraries have great significance in their own countries, because they are usually copyright or legal deposit libraries receiving all published material in their countries. More than this, however, they are frequently the sources of national bibliographies, as well as sometimes acting as agents in the business of international library co-operation.

There are three institutions ranking as national libraries in the United Kingdom – the British Museum Library, the National Library of Scotland, and the National Library of Wales. Curiously enough, there is no national library for England alone as the British Museum Library performs that function for the whole of the United Kingdom.

The British Museum Library is financed by the Treasury and by endowments and, like many British institutions, it has had a chequered growth and existence. Its history began in 1753 when Sir Hans Sloane offered his priceless collection of books and manuscripts to the nation for the sum of £20,000. Fortunately for posterity, Parliament accepted this offer and at

the same time made arrangements to purchase the Harleian
MSS. The British Museum's first home was in Piccadilly, but in
1823 that noted patron of the arts George IV (formerly the
Prince Regent) gave his father's library, now known as the
King's Library, to the country, and the British Museum moved
to its present site in Bloomsbury.

Many extensions have been made to that first building and
now it houses one of the world's greatest libraries, possessing
over seven million volumes in the Department of Printed Books
alone, 38,000 sets of newspapers, over 900,000 musical publications, over 200,000 maps, 100,000 charters and rolls, 10,000
incunabula (i.e. books printed before the year 1500), as well as
large numbers of prints and other material. The *Report of the
National Libraries Committee* (Cmnd. 4028) issued in 1969,
stated that 'the stock of the library extends to about 120 miles
of shelving'.

The library of the British Museum is organized in four
departments – Printed Books; Manuscripts; Oriental Printed
Books and Manuscripts; and Prints and Drawings. In addition,
there is a separate British Museum Newspaper Library,
situated at Colindale, London, NW9 5HE, and there is now the
National Reference Library of Science and Invention, which
has two divisions, one at Holborn and one at Bayswater.

The BML is a copyright library, meaning that under the
Copyright Acts it receives by law a presentation copy of every
publication issued in the United Kingdom. This is to ensure
that copies of all printed publications will be preserved for
posterity. The library is classified according to its own system,
and is catalogued according to its own rules which were
originally formulated and printed in 1839. The BML has produced many catalogues of its stocks of books, as well as catalogues of its maps, plans, charts, music and MSS. The General
Catalogue of Printed Books, which had been in arrears, was
brought up-to-date, reproduced by a photographic process,
and published in 270 volumes between the years 1959 and 1966.
A compact edition of this was prepared and issued by the
Readex Microprint Corporation in 27 volumes in 1967. In 1968
the BML issued the first of a projected ten-yearly series of supplements to the General Catalogue. This was in 50 volumes and
covered the years 1956 to 1965.

The BML has a rapidly growing photographic service and it also houses the State Paper Room, though part of this collection is outhoused at Woolwich. The Reading Room is open to the public but prior application must be made for a reader's ticket. Owing to the very heavy demands made upon reading room space, applications are only granted if the reader's research cannot be carried out elsewhere. No material is lent from the BML.

The BML is also a constituent partner in the enterprise known as the *British National Bibliography* (BNB), and for several years it provided facilities and accommodation for this activity. As space problems grew at the British Museum, BNB obtained other premises in central London and at the time of writing its headquarters are in Rathbone Street, WIP 2AL. Further reference to BNB will be made later in this chapter, when mention is made of the *Report of the National Libraries Committee* (Cmnd. 4028).

Prior to that, some reference must be made to national library provision for Scotland and Wales. The National Library of Scotland is at Edinburgh. It was originally the Library of the Faculty of Advocates, being founded as such in 1682. Its privilege of copyright deposit dates back to 1709. It was given to the nation by the Faculty of Advocates in 1925 and was reconstituted, under a Board of Trustees, by the National Library of Scotland Act of that year. Now the library contains more than three million printed books and MSS., as well as much material relating to Scottish history and families, on which it of course specializes. Its reconstructed building was opened by Queen Elizabeth II in 1956.

Its catalogues are in card, not printed, form, and its reference facilities are supported by a good photocopying service. The question of producing a printed catalogue is being pursued, and it is also hoped to provide a separate reading room for the 3,700 current periodicals which are taken.

The National Library of Wales is much younger than the other two national libraries in Great Britain. It is situated at Aberystwyth and, while it was first mooted in 1873, it was not inaugurated until 1909. It now contains over two million printed books including periodicals and newspapers, as well as over 30,000 volumes of MSS, and about three and a half million deeds and other documents. Naturally, it is rich in Welsh and Celtic material, and it is one of the six libraries to benefit under the Copyright Act of 1911. Only certain classes of books may, however, be demanded by the National Library of Wales.

A Court of Governors is responsible for the Library, which obtains its finances from a Government grant-in-aid administered through the Welsh Office. Numerous catalogues have been issued by the Library which, incidentally, is classified according to the Library of Congress scheme. Like the other British national libraries, it has a photographic department producing photocopies and microforms. It also acts as one of the two regional library bureaux for Wales.

Two other libraries with the word 'national' in their style and title must be briefly mentioned here, though they are treated in greater detail in chapter 4. These are the National Central Library, and the National Library for Science and Technology. The National Central Library, or NCL, began its existence in 1916 as the Central Library for Students, and it did not get its present title until 1930. Its original aim was to facilitate the supply of books to students in adult education classes, but as time has passed, it has become more important as the centre for interlibrary loans in England and Wales. It also lends from its own stock, and acts as the British centre for international library loans.

The National Lending Library for Science and Technology (NLLST, sometimes abbreviated to NLL) for some years operated as the DSIR Lending Library Unit auxiliary to the Science Museum Library. In 1962 however the NLL began to occupy a site at Boston Spa in Yorkshire, and was officially inaugurated there in November of that year. The main purpose of the NLL is 'to supplement the internal library resources of existing organisations by providing a rapid loan service'. Some of the Science Library's stock was transferred to the NLL and this was supplemented from other sources. Although many books are included in its stock, it relies mainly on its vast and increasing holdings of scientific and technical periodicals, culled from all over the world. Much microform material is also held, and photocopies of articles are promptly supplied.

These two libraries, the NCL and the NLL, are briefly introduced here for a special reason. This is because the *Report of the*

National Libraries Committee (Cmnd. 4028) included them in its recommendations to the Government on future policy for the national libraries. The whole of this Report is recommended reading, but its recommendations are summarized on pages xii to xv of Cmnd. 4028. They are not repeated here because they are superseded by a Government White Paper (Cmnd. 4572) which was issued in January 1971.

In this White Paper, entitled *The British Library*, the Government proposed to combine the BML, the NRLSI, the NCL, the NLL and the BNB into a single organization to be called the British Library. The objectives of this British Library include:

(*a*) preserving and making available for reference at least one copy of every book and periodical of domestic origin and of as many overseas publications as possible.

(*b*) providing an efficient central lending and photocopying service in support of the other libraries and information systems of the country.

(*c*) providing central cataloguing and other bibliographic services related not only to the needs of the central libraries but to those of libraries and information centres throughout the country and in close co-operation with central libraries overseas.

The Government recognized the need for expanding libraries to be rehoused. The BML, including the NRLSI, will have a new building to the south of the existing British Museum, while the NLL at Boston Spa will also be extended. 'The operations', said the White Paper, 'will therefore be centred on two complexes, one for reference, research and bibliographical services in London, and one for lending services at Boston Spa.'

It is made clear in the White Paper that the National Libraries of Scotland and Wales, the Science Museum Library and other libraries of national importance will stay independent of the British Library. It is further intended that the British Library shall be governed by a Board of not more than twelve members, some of whom will be full-time, but the majority will be part-time members. The Chairman of the Board will probably be a full-time appointment. Finance for the British Library will come from an annual grant-in-aid from the Department of Education and Science.

The NRLSI is to be renamed the Science Reference Library,

and it is intended to organize the British Library in four separate directorates, one for the BML, one for the Science Reference Library, one for the Bibliographic Services, and one for the Lending Services. For each directorate an Advisory Council will be appointed to ensure that account is taken of users' needs. It is possible that the directorate for Lending Services may be divided into two, one section for the humanities and social sciences, and the other for science and technology. In any event the main operations of the NCL will be transferred to Boston Spa as soon as possible.

There are other and more detailed intentions, and study should be made of Cmnd. 4572 itself. The White Paper ends by saying that 'the result will be the creation of a national library system without rival' and that London will eventually have the most significant complex of museums and library resources in Europe.

UNIVERSITY LIBRARIES

It has long been recognized that universities must have the best possible libraries as aids in their work of advanced education, and it can be asserted confidently that the universities of Great Britain have generally got good libraries. Normally university libraries are open only to members and students of the universities, but their resources are often made available to any bona fide research worker who cannot find his information elsewhere. The chief users of university libraries are, of course, the undergraduates, the faculties, and those engaged in postgraduate research. The older university libraries such as the Bodleian at Oxford and the Cambridge University Library do not normally lend books, because borrowing facilities are provided by the libraries of the colleges within the university. In Scotland however, as well as in the newer English universities, borrowing facilities are provided.

Since the last edition of this book appeared a *Report of the Committee on Libraries* has been issued, published in 1967 for the University Grants Committee by HMSO. Although dealing basically with university libraries, and containing many recommendations for their future development, the Report

2

could not avoid making generous reference to national library services and library co-operation. Because of this, it may be regarded as the forerunner of the *Report of the National Libraries Committee* (Cmnd. 4028), and it will repay careful reading.

In addition to its factual content and its many positive recommendations relating to university libraries, the *Report of the Committee on Libraries* contains many statistical tables and other supplementary matter of great value. Unfortunately, the statistics were not very up-to-date even when they were printed, since they refer to the year 1964–5. Nevertheless, they are indicative of the varied sizes and total strength of British university libraries, and more current figures are obtainable from *Statistics of Education*, vol. 6, published annually for the Department of Education and Science by HMSO.

The Report's figures show that British universities possessed in 1964–5 nearly 20,000,000 bound volumes, and nearly 38,000 reader places. By far the largest university libraries are those of London, with nearly four million bound volumes, the Bodleian Library, with over 3,200,000 volumes and Cambridge University Library, with just over three million volumes. No other British university library had at that time more than a million books in stock.

The Bodleian Library at Oxford dates from the fourteenth century, although it was not until 1598 that Sir Thomas Bodley rescued the collection from disrepute and founded its present greatness. Since then it has grown steadily and in 1946 King George VI opened the extended premises, which are designed to be large enough to house the library for the next two hundred years. It is a copyright library but, unlike the BML, it does not *automatically* receive a copy of every new publication. It may apply to the publishers for a copy under the Copyright Act, and if it does so the publisher must by law supply a copy. The Bodleian has its own scheme of classification and its own code of cataloguing. It has published printed catalogues of parts of its stock, and it also issues a staff manual for the routine guidance of its personnel.

The origins of the Cambridge University Library go far back into antiquity. There is evidence of a library before 1400, but it was not until well into the fifteenth century that it was really firmly established. Through the centuries there was much neglect and the library lacked a Bodley to give it the standing and importance of its counterpart at Oxford. Over the years it did, however, receive many valuable bequests and it has been a copyright library since before the passing of the first Copyright Act in 1709. In addition to its stock of over three million volumes, it possesses 12,000 MSS, and about 400,000 maps. Among its treasures is the Codex Bezae, a manuscript copy of Bede's *Ecclesiastical History of the English People*, eight manuscript registers of the Benedictine Abbey of Bury St Edmunds, the Acton historical library and the Bradshaw collection of Irish books and pamphlets. In 1934 it was housed in an imposing new building designed by Sir Giles Gilbert Scott and opened by King George V.

The libraries of the Scottish universities of Aberdeen, Edinburgh, Glasgow and St Andrews are all old-established and have collections of national importance. One reason for this is that they all benefited under the Copyright Act of 1709 although they are no longer ranked as copyright deposit libraries. Aberdeen now has nearly half a million volumes including several important special collections; Glasgow possesses over 800,000 volumes and MSS including the Hunterian collection; St Andrews University Library has been in its present premises since 1642 and is rich in early printed books and MSS; while Edinburgh University Library's collection of about a million volumes is now rehoused in a striking new building of over 20,000 square metres designed by the eminent architect Sir Basil Spence.

In London the main University Library is housed in a building in Malet Street which was erected in the 1930s. Its stock includes many celebrated special collections such as Goldsmith's library of economics, the Durning-Lawrence Library on Bacon and Shakespeare, and the Harry Price Library on psychical phenomena and magic. In the provinces there are important university libraries at Birmingham, Leeds, Liverpool and Manchester.

There has been a great expansion in the field of university librarianship in Great Britain consequent upon the many new universities which have been established up and down the country in the 1960s and since. Among these new universities are those of East Anglia, Essex, Keele, Lancaster, Sussex,

Warwick and York. The setting-up of libraries for these new universities has created many opportunities, challenges and problems for the profession. It has meant an immediate expansion in both the professional and non-professional sides of librarianship, and it has also given the opportunity of planning many new buildings. Not many years ago British university libraries had little to show in library architecture, but with the recent buildings opened at the Universities of Sussex, York, Kent, Warwick and elsewhere, the situation is now improved.

The most challenging and difficult task in the new university libraries has been building up stocks of books and ancillary materials. The task of assembling large numbers of basic books often published many years ago calls for great bibliographical knowledge and resource, as well as patience. In most cases good starts have been made, though it will be many years before some of these newer university libraries will be able to boast of really adequate stocks and, of course, it is unlikely that they will ever catch up with the libraries at the older-established universities.

Reference has already been made to the University Grants Committee's *Report of the Committee on Libraries*, published by HMSO in 1967, and this remains essential reading for students of library science. The Report, known as the Parry Report after the name of the Committee's chairman, made many recommendations which are summarized on pages 157 to 164. Some of these recommendations have already been realized either as written or near enough to satisfy university librarians; others are still under consideration and may take longer to achieve.

Those who work in university libraries find that they can learn much from their colleagues overseas, because organizational and administrative problems are not always altered by national frontiers. It was most encouraging to note, by the way, that the Parry Committee took much cognisance of overseas university library practice and experience when preparing its Report.

Some splendid examples of university libraries can be found in many parts of the world, particularly in the United States of America, but also in Canada, Australia and other parts of the

English-speaking world. The complex of libraries on the various campuses of the University of California are the admiration of all who visit them, for their architecture, contents and administration. Among other notable American university libraries are the vast collections at Yale and Harvard, as well as the university libraries of Illinois at Urbana, of Michigan at Ann Arbor, and many others.

In Europe, German university libraries are to the fore, while another important one is the Moscow University Library situated on the Lenin Hills just outside the centre of the city. In Scandinavia, as the Parry Report pointed out: 'the libraries of Oslo and Helsinki Universities have become the national libraries of their respective countries, while the opposite trend is seen at work in Stockholm and Copenhagen, where the Royal Libraries are adding to their function as national libraries those of university libraries'. Scandinavia is generally a fount of good architecture and design, and there are notable recent buildings housing the university libraries at Århus in Denmark, Bergen in Norway, Gothenburg in Sweden and Tampere in Finland. It is never too early for the student librarian to be apprised of university library development overseas, and every effort should be made to make as many visits as possible.

UNIVERSITY COLLEGE LIBRARIES

University colleges invariably possess libraries, but these are of several types. The colleges of Oxford and Cambridge, being old institutions, are rich in early printed books, MSS, and older material generally. They have also benefited in the past from bequests and donations, and among their special collections are to be found such treasures as the Pepys' Library in Magdalene College, Cambridge, and the Goodyer botanical collection in Magdalene College, Oxford. A great part of the stock of these older college libraries is obviously set aside for reference and research purposes only, but undergraduate collections are also maintained.

Colleges of other universities have libraries which are generally intended for the use of faculties and undergraduates.

Some of the colleges of the University of London are quite old-established and as a result their libraries are large and important collections. Among these may be mentioned those of University College, King's College, Strand, Birkbeck College, Royal Holloway College, Bedford College and Queen Mary College. In the provinces there are notable university college libraries at Aberystwyth, Bangor, Cardiff, Londonderry, Manchester, Newcastle upon Tyne, St Andrews and Swansea.

SPECIAL LIBRARIES

The term *special libraries* has been in use for a number of years to denote specialist libraries, that is, those specializing on a certain subject or group of subjects. As a generic term it is rather unsatisfactory as it includes a number of different kinds of libraries, such as those of commercial and industrial concerns, Government departments, learned societies, research associations, professional associations and corporate bodies of many sorts. An attempt will be made in the succeeding paragraphs to differentiate briefly between these various types.

It was in the 1920s that industry and commerce woke up to the fact that the rapidly changing technological scene necessitated more detailed and specific library and information services for their staffs than the average public library could possibly afford to give. The research library of Kodak Ltd was, for example, founded at Wealdstone in 1928; the various branches of Imperial Chemical Industries have research libraries originating from various dates since the late 1920s; the Bristol Aeroplane Company, the Metal Box Company, and Richard Thomas and Baldwins Ltd are all examples of the many industrial and commercial firms which have set up libraries and information services within their organizations.

The Second World War, which spurred technological advances in many areas, resulted in a great expansion in the number of companies inaugurating their own library services. In the main, this type of special library is designed for research and information needs and is used only by the personnel of the organization concerned, although many such libraries co-operate with others through their regions or as Outliers with the

National Central Library. As they are often concerned with 'micro-thought', that is, supplying very detailed and highly specialized information, their stock consists more of journals, documents, cuttings, illustrations and other fugitive material than it does of books, though books, especially foreign titles, are an important part of their resources.

The journals taken usually include many in foreign languages, and important articles are translated, abstracted and indexed. The staffs of industrial libraries are often small in number, though examples exist with larger and highly qualified staffs, but they have to be expert in providing research workers with the specialist information they require. The enormous spread of industrial libraries since the Second World War is obviously due to the fact that the librarians and information officers of the older-established ones did noteworthy work and made themselves indispensable. The great increase in technological literature since 1945 has also been an influencing factor in the expansion of this type of library.

GOVERNMENT LIBRARIES

In addition to the BML, the Government is responsible for many libraries through its various departments and agencies. One category of these may be perhaps described as branches of the national libraries. These include the Science Museum Library, and the libraries of such institutions as the Victoria and Albert Museum, the Geological Museum and the National Maritime Museum. The most important, if not the largest of these, are the Science Museum Library and that of the Victoria and Albert Museum, the latter being the national art library. In fact it is now referred to as the British Library of Art.

The Science Museum Library has over 400,000 volumes, almost 20,000 files of journals, and an extensive collection in microforms. It is classified according to the Universal Decimal Classification, and lends material to approved institutions. A fuller account of its functions and services may be found in the *Report of the National Libraries Committee* (Cmnd. 4028) on pages 38 to 44.

The British Library of Art at the Victoria and Albert

Museum is also mentioned in Cmnd. 4028, though only briefly on pages 75 and 76. This collection also has over 400,000 volumes, though for reference only. It is administered by the Department of Education and Science, and the Dainton Committee was of the opinion that its future administration should be the subject of further examination.

Other libraries administered by the Government are those of the Whitehall departments such as the Ministry of Defence, the Foreign Office and other ministries and departments. Like the special libraries of industry these have been developed enormously during the last few decades. These departmental libraries obviously tend to be special libraries, though they also contain background material of a general character. Their main purpose is, of course, to provide information for the Minister, his senior civil servants, and the staff of the department generally, but many will serve outside research workers on application, and a few will lend material through the NCL or sometimes direct to other libraries.

Another type of Government library is that attached to a national research organization such as the National Institute for Medical Research. Then there are the libraries of the House of Commons and the House of Lords, but these are private collections for members of Parliament and are not open to the public either for reference or for lending. Mention must also be made of the British Council libraries which are maintained in many overseas cities and centres. These are not for the purpose of disseminating political propaganda, indeed they contain a minimum of books on politics. On the other hand, they do try to present the British way of life and to this end they are strong on British institutions and literature, especially contemporary poetry, prose, drama and fiction. The British Council libraries have had a chequered history, reflecting home economic conditions to a large extent. During the Second World War and just afterwards, expenditure on them rose steadily, but severe cuts have taken place from time to time since then. At one time the Library Association had to urge the Government to ensure that more of the British Council libraries were put in the charge of chartered librarians, but these representations had a good effect.

Of course Britain is not the only country which organizes

cultural libraries of this kind in foreign cities. The American libraries are especially noteworthy, although cuts in financial aid caused closures, notably of the excellent example in London's Grosvenor Square. Where they still exist, the American libraries, such as those in Oslo and Bucharest, are valuable sources of information on the American way of life, and use of them is free to all who reside in the countries where they are located. Although not an American library in this sense, mention must be made here of the American Memorial Library (*Gedenkbibliothek*) in West Berlin, which houses a general collection of books and other materials in a striking building.

As well as the British Council and American libraries, many capital cities all over the world have libraries organized by bodies which exist to explain and further various national cultures. Examples of such bodies are the German Institute, the Danish Institute, L'Institut Français and the Swedish Institute for Cultural Affairs.

LIBRARIES OF LEARNED SOCIETIES AND CORPORATE BODIES

As with Government departments and industrial firms, most learned societies, professional associations and corporate bodies have found it essential to set up libraries and information bureaux to cope with the increasing volume of literature. The great majority of British societies and associations have their headquarters in London, but the provincial cities have their share of this type of library. Examples are the libraries of the Royal Society of Medicine, the Institute of Transport, the British Dental Association, the National Book League and the Library Association. Their aim is, of course, to collect as much material as possible on their subjects, and to supply information for their members by post, telephone, Telex or in person. British and foreign books and journals are collected and preserved, as are photographs, newscuttings, slides, filmstrips, films, letters, autographs and other documentary materials.

In this type of library the vertical files often contain as much material as the shelves: sometimes they are used even more than the shelves. Those students who live near London should visit the Library Association library and study its layout and contents, for it gives a good idea of what a professional or society library should be like. A list of such libraries can be found in the *Aslib Directory* or in the *Libraries, Museums and Art Galleries Year Book*. These lists should be studied, if only to give the student an impression of the many such collections that exist.

LIBRARIES IN POLYTECHNICS AND COLLEGES OF EDUCATION

The organization and structure of technical education in Britain has changed rapidly in the last year or two, and this is having its effect upon libraries in colleges of technology. In any event, the development of libraries and librarianship in technical colleges is fairly recent. Before the Second World War only the very largest technical colleges had libraries and these were rarely in the charge of chartered librarians. Since then, the position has improved and most colleges have libraries of considerable size and importance, and more of them are in the charge of qualified librarians.

It is intended to concentrate courses of higher education in about thirty institutions in England and Wales, to be known as Polytechnics, and most of these have now been established. Some of the new Polytechnics have been based on existing institutions, others have been formed by merging together several neighbouring technical colleges. Speaking generally, this is a welcome development from the library standpoint, for it means a garnering together of different resources to form stronger, more viable and more effective collections. It permits also the employment of many more chartered librarians who are already working hard to merge the constituent libraries and to organize them on the best professional lines.

The Library Association published standards of library provision for colleges of technology and other establishments of further education in 1965 in a publication entitled *College Libraries*, this really being the third edition of standards which had previously been issued in 1957 with a second edition in 1959. In the light of the recent developments in technological education these are again being revised.

Newer still than librarianship in technical colleges is librarianship in colleges of education, those institutions which were formerly called training colleges. There are about 150 colleges of education in Great Britain and they all possess libraries or at least working collections of books. In 1961 the Library Association and the Association of Teachers in Colleges and Departments of Education jointly produced a memorandum on the development of training college libraries, and in 1967 the two bodies issued *College of Education Libraries: Recommended Standards for their Development.* It is plain that, although the first memorandum had a beneficial effect, there is still a long way to go before all the colleges of education in the country achieve the required minimum standards.

The best college principals have, however, always recognized the need for chartered librarians and their employment in this field is happily growing. Although chiefly concerned with education and teaching techniques, these libraries generally contain standard books on subjects in the educational curriculum, as well as general reference books. Liaison with public libraries in the vicinity is essential, so that books can be borrowed through the recognized schemes of library co-operation. The post of college of education librarian is now recognized to be a full-time one, unencumbered by tutorial work other than that connected with bibliography and the use and resources of the library.

NEWSPAPER, RADIO AND TV LIBRARIES

Another type of library which has grown up is the newspaper library. By this we do not mean an organization such as the British Museum Newspaper Library at Colindale, which is a repository for storing newspapers of all kinds, but the working library which is attached to some of the national or provincial daily newspapers. Such collections are indeed *working* libraries in the strict sense of the term, for they exist to provide quick information for editors, sub-editors and journalists who require facts in a hurry. Books form only a part of these libraries, the majority of the material comprising pamphlets, press cuttings, photographs, maps, blocks, negatives, microfilm and bound copies of other newspapers. The emphasis, as well as being on speed, is on the production of up-to-date information. More often than not it is the speech, or the report of the day before, which is quickly required. Furthermore, as the library has to be open all hours of the day and night, the files and information have to be organized on a self-service basis, as the library staff cannot be present all the time. Not all newspaper libraries are in the charge of chartered librarians, but recognition of professional qualifications is on the increase.

In much the same category as newspaper libraries are the increasing number of collections owned by radio and TV corporations all over the world. In the United Kingdom the most substantial of these is owned by the British Broadcasting Corporation. This is not just one library but many, for in addition to the headquarters collection at Broadcasting House there are other collections such as that at the Television Centre at Shepherd's Bush, and those in the various BBC regions. Commercial TV in the United Kingdom also has its own libraries, and so, of course, do most radio and TV organizations wherever they may be. The *raison d'être* of these libraries is to provide information for programme editors, producers and indeed all who work for the organization. The growth of television has meant that such libraries must concentrate more upon pictorial records, though books and journals in large numbers are still the basic need. The BBC, for example, possesses the Radio Times Hulton Picture Library, and TV viewers will not need reminding how often this appears in the credit titles of BBC television programmes. Co-operation with other libraries is essential, and radio and TV libraries lean heavily upon the public libraries, which are glad to give all possible help.

SCHOOL LIBRARIES AND RESOURCE CENTRES

The importance of libraries in schools is universally recognized and it is probably true to say that every school possesses a library of some kind or other. It is also true to say that some are more effective than others, for the stage has not yet been reached where all schools in the United Kingdom have libraries which come up to the required minimum standards.

School libraries, which increasingly are becoming part of the larger activity known as resource centres, are usually in the charge of part-time teacher-librarians and a great deal depends upon their enthusiasm and ability.

In the larger schools which are becoming more common with the trend towards comprehensive education, it is noticeable that school libraries are being staffed with full-time chartered librarians, and this should surely be the ultimate aim of all school libraries. In the United Kingdom there has been little or no national direction, and in the absence too of any published standards, school libraries have compared badly with their counterparts in the United States, Canada, Australia and some of the Scandinavian countries. To remedy this unstable situation, the Library Association set up a School Libraries Sub-Committee in 1969, and in the following year the Association published *School Library Resource Centres: Recommended Standards for Policy and Provision.*

This publication, which was widely circulated to education and library authorities, was generally welcomed and there are positive signs already of its good effect. It studied the problem in its entirety, and after describing the purpose and function of the school library, it gave useful advice on the administration, organization and finance, and set out minimum standards for staffing, accommodation and stocks of books and other materials necessary in different types and sizes of schools. Some education authorities had already achieved some of these goals, but the majority fell short by a long way. The influence of these Library Association approved standards is now beginning to be felt, and expansion of school libraries is certain to take place in the immediate future.

Chapter 2
Public libraries

Most countries now have public library systems, though they range from the highly developed to the embryo type. There are also great differences in the administration and organization of public libraries from country to country, though there are increasing similarities in the end-product, that is the service offered to users. We sometimes speak of the Anglo-American-Scandinavian concept of the public library, and this is because there are many common strains in the history and development of public libraries in the United Kingdom, the USA, and the Scandinavian countries. On closer examination, however, we may discover that there are still many divergences, not quite so much in the administration as in the basic organization of their respective public library systems. There are still greater differences to be found if we extend our comparative studies to the state of public librarianship in other parts of the world, say to India, to South Africa, and to the countries of Eastern Europe.

Comparative librarianship is an advanced concept which the student may encounter in his subsequent studies, and it is certainly outside the range of this book. It is only mentioned here in order to convey the basic idea that great care is needed when we are discussing public libraries in general.

Even in the small compass of the United Kingdom there are some differences to note between public libraries in England, Wales, Scotland and Northern Ireland, such divergences being entirely attributable to the effects of both central and local government in the four countries. It is, in fact, necessary to look at the framework of local government in particular if we want to understand the progress of public libraries in the United Kingdom. This will not be easy, the more so since local government is in a state of flux at the time of writing, although its future in England and Wales from 1974 onwards has now been agreed.

Outside Greater London, which in 1965 was divided into thirty-two London boroughs plus the City of London, the local government units have been county councils, county boroughs, municipal boroughs, urban districts, rural districts and parishes. In February 1971, following investigations taking place over a number of years into the structure of local government in England and Wales, a White Paper (Cmnd. 4584) was issued outlining Government proposals for the reorganization of local government in England, and later there was a consultative document dealing with the situation in Wales. From these two publications emanated the Local Government Bill dated November 1971. Later reference will be made to this, and its effects upon public libraries, but it is sufficient to say now that the legislation will abolish the old local government units, setting up in their place just two units to be known as county councils and district councils. But before we examine the inferences of these changes, it is essential to cover the legislative, administrative and organizational processes which have led up to the present public library situation in the United Kingdom.

PUBLIC LIBRARIES ACTS

Public Libraries Acts are, in brief, Parliament's sanction for the setting-up and managing of public rate-supported libraries. Parliament is the fount from which all local government law springs, and Parliamentary Acts of 1850, 1892, 1919 and 1964 (as well as those of other but less important dates) are the authority for the provision, government and financing of public libraries in England and Wales. For Scotland the relevant Acts are those of 1853, 1887 and 1955, with additional powers granted under the Education (Scotland) Act of 1946 and the Local Government (Scotland) Act of 1947. For Northern Ireland, the Acts to be noted are those of 1855 and 1877, together with the Public Libraries (Northern Ireland) Act of 1924.

The campaign for public libraries in England and Wales was fought in the 1840s, the leading protagonists being William Ewart and Joseph Brotherton, who were both members of Parliament, and Edward Edwards, a librarian at the British

Museum. In 1849 a Select Committee on Public Libraries was appointed, Edward Edwards being chiefly responsible for the contents of its report. Following this, Ewart and Brotherton in 1850 piloted the first Public Libraries Bill through the House of Commons, not without opposition from Colonel Sibthorpe and some other members.

The Public Libraries Act of 1850 will always be important as being the first law authorizing the provision of public libraries as we in the United Kingdom know them today. Although the Act was a great step forward, it was also a very hesitant step as it merely allowed town councils of a population of 10,000 and over, if they wished, to provide a library building, a librarian, light and fuel. The Act was thus permissive, but not mandatory. It laid down that admission to public libraries was to be free, but no authority was given for the purchase of books, and no town council could levy a rate of more than one halfpenny in the pound.

The first town to adopt the Act was Norwich which did so in September 1850, although it did not actually provide a service until seven years later. Manchester was the first to provide a library under the Act, starting its service in 1852 with Edward Edwards as its first librarian. Warrington had already been providing a public library service before 1850 in conjunction with its Mechanics' Institute, and Brighton had also been operating a service in 1850 under a local Act of Parliament chiefly concerned with the Royal Pavilion. Other towns quick to adopt the Act were Blackburn, Bolton, Cambridge, Ipswich, Liverpool, Oxford, Sheffield and Winchester. London at that period was governed by many small Vestry Councils, and the first public library to appear in London was in 1857 after the Parish of St Margaret and St John adopted the Act and opened a library in Great Smith Street in the present City of Westminster.

The 1850 Act applied only to England and Wales, and powers were not extended to Scotland and Ireland until 1853. It very soon became obvious that the law of 1850, though well intentioned, was quite inadequate. Fortunately its limitations did not last long, and in 1855 a brief Amendment Act was passed, granting powers to public library authorities for the purchase of books and at the same time permitting the expenditure on public libraries to be increased from a rate of one halfpenny in the pound to one penny in the pound. This rate limit, which became more crippling as the years passed by, persisted until 1919.

Subsequently further amending Acts were passed by Parliament, altering certain clauses in the 1850 law and making additional provisions. Eventually the important Public Libraries Act of 1892 was passed. This was a consolidating Act, which is one that gathers the still relevant provisions of previous Acts, adds new legislation, and becomes the principal Act, making all previous laws redundant and of historical value only.

In 1919, another Public Libraries Act was passed, the main provisions of which were the abolition of the penny rate limitation in England and Wales, and the permission given to county councils to set up their own public library services. The former amendment removed the shackles which had stunted public library development since 1855, and public library authorities were at last free to spend as much money as they wished. The second provision, that which allowed the establishment of county libraries, attempted to provide for rural areas the same library facilities as were possible in the towns and urban areas. The 1919 Act laid down that county councils could adopt the Public Libraries Acts for the whole or any part of the county, except those parts which were already library authorities at the time of the county adoption.

Between 1919 and 1964 public library law in England and Wales was slightly affected by minor clauses in Acts devoted to the larger fields of local government and education. In Scotland, however, there was a major change when the Public Libraries (Scotland) Act was passed in 1955. This removed the threepenny rate limitation on public library expenditure in that country. It also legalized library co-operation in Scotland and provided for the financing of the Scottish Central Library partly by the Government and partly by local authorities. In addition the Act allowed authorities to revoke adoption of the Public Libraries Consolidation (Scotland) Act, 1887, and authorized the lending of material other than books.

The progress of public libraries in England and Wales after 1919 was phenomenal, and another main Public Libraries Act

3

became overdue. There was no lack of suggestions on the topic of public library reform during the period. In 1927 a Board of Education Committee on Public Libraries issued a document known as the Kenyon Report, and this was the motivating force behind the development of the schemes of library co-operation to be described in a later chapter (see p. 55). In 1942 L. R. McColvin made a comprehensive survey of the public library services of the United Kingdom, and in his report he called for a national library service, offering strong evidence to show that many of the smaller library authorities of that time did not possess the necessary financial resources to maintain efficient library services. But the McColvin Report was in no way an official document and it was certainly not called for by the Government of the day.

Fifteen years later, in 1957, the Minister of Education set up a committee under the chairmanship of Sir Sydney Roberts to report upon the structure of the public library service in England and Wales. This committee issued its report in February 1959 as Cmnd. 660, and it made many recommenda-tions, some of which had been foreshadowed by the unofficial McColvin Report. Its main proposal was that the provision by local authorities of an efficient library service should be a statutory duty, and that the Minister of Education should be responsible for its supervision, aided by two advisory bodies, one for England and one for Wales. It also made important com-ments upon the minimum size of library authorities, suggesting 50,000 population as the lower limit.

The Roberts Report, as it quickly became known, was the subject of animated discussion on all sides, and after receiving comments on it from interested bodies, the Minister of Educa-tion set up two Working Parties to advise him on the detail of future legislation based on the Roberts Committee's conclu-sions. In December 1962 these Working Party reports were issued separately under the titles of *Inter-Library Co-operation in England and Wales* and *Standards of Public Library Service in England and Wales*. The first of these is mentioned again in a later chapter (see p. 61). The second offered no fewer than seventy-eight recommendations on public library standards, many of which were generalizations but others provided specific figures relating to stock, staff and buildings, below which no library should operate. The Working Party collected detailed figures from over seventy library authorities of varying sizes, and these were included in the Report as appendices.

These three Reports, that of the Roberts Committee and the two Working Party Reports, were acted upon in 1964 when Parliament passed the Public Libraries and Museums Act of that year. This twenty-six clause law superseded all previous public library legislation for England and Wales, and has thus become the main Act.

The 1964 Act followed most, though not all, of the guidance offered by the Reports. Briefly it made an efficient public library service mandatory and made the Secretary of State responsible for its supervision and improvement throughout England and Wales. It created two Library Advisory Councils one for England, and the other for Wales and Monmouthshire. It designated as library authorities county councils, county borough councils, London borough councils and the Common Council of the City of London. Non-county boroughs and urban districts were allowed to remain library authorities if they were already operating services. The Act did not follow the advice of the Roberts Committee in its suggestion of 50,000 population as the minimum for an efficient service. Instead, the figure of 40,000 population is given in the Act, and the Secretary of State was given powers to revoke the adoption of the Act by local authorities of less than this population if, after consultations 'he is of opinion that to do so would lead to an improvement in the library facilities . . . in the borough or urban district'.

In fact the Secretary of State has not found it necessary to do this. Consideration was deferred in the light of the local government reorganization, but there have been noticeable reductions in the number of library authorities. These have been due to limited local government reorganizations such as took place at Teesside, Torbay, Warley and elsewhere, and the other cause of the reduction was that a number of smaller library authorities voluntarily relinquished their powers to the county councils, since they realized they would obtain a better service by doing so.

The Act went on to emphasize that it was a duty of every library authority to provide a comprehensive and efficient service, and a special point was made of the need to encourage both adults and children to make full use of the service. Specific mention was made of the fact that no charge was to be made for the borrowing of a book, journal, pamphlet or similar article, but the way was left open for libraries to charge for the borrowing of gramophone records if the authority so wished. This latter point was against the strongest possible advice from the Roberts Committee.

There are, of course, other detailed clauses in the 1964 Act, to which students are referred.

Now we must return to the proposals for local government reorganization in England and Wales, to which earlier reference was made. The Local Government Bill states that the intention is that in England the only library authorities shall be the councils of non-metropolitan counties, the councils of metropolitan districts, and the councils of London boroughs plus the Common Council of the City of London. This intention has now been enacted, and the proposals for boundary changes will reduce the number of library authorities in England to 105, since there are going to be 38 county councils, 34 metropolitan district councils, and 33 councils in Greater London.

This is entirely in accordance with the advice consistently offered by the Library Association, and means that not only will all the new library authorities be of a size capable of maintaining efficient services, but also, apart from Inner London, the new library authorities will be coincidental with education authorities. This is a most desirable link.

PUBLIC LIBRARY DEVELOPMENT

Despite the faults in their past structure, public library services have developed steadily and continue to develop. For national coverage it is perhaps second to none in the world, since every inhabitant of the United Kingdom has ready access to a service. In the fields of administration, staff, book stock and ancillary services only the United States and some of the Commonwealth and Scandinavian countries rival British practice.

The most outstanding drawback over the years has been the lack of suitable premises. Many of the older British public library buildings were erected with the financial assistance of the benefactor Andrew Carnegie. For present-day librarianship they are totally inadequate, but this is not to detract from the generosity of Carnegie, without which the position would be much worse than it is today. The Roberts Report pointed out that the country's capital expenditure on public library buildings had for many years been insufficient. Since that Report appeared in 1958 there has been a signal improvement, and hundreds of new buildings have been erected in many parts of the United Kingdom. The majority of these have, however, been branch libraries, many of them quite small, and while some progress has been made in the provision of new main libraries in cities, towns and counties, a great deal remains to be done in this area.

RANGE OF SERVICES PROVIDED

Public library systems are now fairly standardized throughout the United Kingdom, though there is still a gulf between the best and the worst. This gulf has narrowed noticeably since the appearance of the Roberts Report and the passing of the 1964 Act. The Library Advisory Councils set up under that Act have perhaps had a greater influence on this than might be imagined.

In the smallest systems there is usually one library in the centre of the area served, and this building contains all the essential departments – home reading library, reference and information library, children's and youth library, and periodicals room. Some do not have separate reference libraries, having integrated their lending and reference stocks into subject divisions. There will also, of course, be offices, work and staff rooms, stores for attendants, and space for reserve stock. In larger areas the main library is augmented by branch libraries, which may vary considerably in their size and scope. Branches, in fact, range from small, part-time premises to the large suburban branch which is often as big as, or bigger than, a small town main library. Mobile libraries, common in county areas, are also used in some urban systems.

Gramophone record libraries have become a common feature,

while in recent years public librarians have devoted more attention to the needs of the aged and physically handicapped members of the community by the organization and provision of services to the housebound. Many public libraries in the United Kingdom also organize school and hospital library provision in their areas, though these services are by no means universal.

Dealing for the moment with urban library systems, it would be invidious to select good examples for special mention when the majority of them conform to a reasonable standard. For the guidance of students, however, a few must be mentioned, and of the largest systems Liverpool, Manchester, Sheffield and Glasgow are prominent, while Birmingham has a new central library to show. Newcastle upon Tyne and Bradford also have recent main libraries as well as some interesting branches. Luton, with its main library opened in 1964, plus branches, mobiles, schools and hospitals service, has been an admirable example of a medium-sized system, while the London Borough of Barnet is a good instance of a suburban system with many well-sited branches.

Apart from the new main libraries already mentioned, the last decade or so has witnessed the appearance of new main libraries at Doncaster, Grimsby, Eastbourne, Crosby, Bebington, Stoke-on-Trent, Nuneaton, Norwich and other towns, while new branch libraries in cities and towns are now very numerous.

COUNTY LIBRARIES

As already mentioned, county libraries were not authorized until 1919, but in their short existence the county authorities tackled their problems with such energy that there are now no rural areas, however remote, without a library service. The Carnegie United Kingdom Trust (CUKT) played a large part in the initiation and development of county libraries, having provided the original impetus, and having given generous grants to the systems in their early days.

County libraries have operated from a headquarters normally, but not always, situated near the county council offices in the county town. Some of these headquarters began merely as clearing-houses where books were selected, ordered, catalogued and despatched to the various branches and centres throughout the county. The public was not usually admitted to such a headquarters, but over the years the concept has changed. Some county library headquarters began to include reference or students' sections, but the latest examples have gone further and usually include a public department to serve the community in which the headquarters is situated.

As the county library has had to supply books throughout its area to such widely differing communities as large towns, villages, hamlets and scattered rural areas, it has used diverse methods to attain its objectives. Towns are usually served by full-time branch libraries such as those at Crawley in West Sussex, or Hitchin in Hertfordshire. Indeed the county libraries have been most active in providing new buildings. New, purpose-built county library headquarters have been erected for Kent, Durham, Flintshire, Montgomeryshire, Zetland and elsewhere. In the field of branch libraries most counties have much to show, but special mention ought to be made of Cheshire, Lancashire, Buckinghamshire, Hertford-shire, Nottinghamshire, West Sussex, Warwickshire and Lanarkshire.

In short, county library development in the United Kingdom has been a success story, achieved in a relatively short time. Fuller details may be found in a short survey entitled *British County Libraries, 1919–1969*, edited by K. A. Stockham, which was prepared to celebrate the fiftieth anniversary of their establishment.

Now, with local government reorganization in the offing, the county libraries in England and Wales must prepare to sink their present identities and merge with other library systems in their areas. This may be regretted by some, but the changes present challenges and opportunities. Experience gained in the amalgamations of the London boroughs in 1965 and after showed that if careful preparations are made, many of the difficulties of merging public library systems are capable of short-term solutions. Obviously there are other problems which can only be met in the long term, but given the will to succeed, the barometer seems to be set fair for an exciting redevelopment

of public libraries in the United Kingdom during the last
quarter of the twentieth century.

PUBLIC LIBRARIES OVERSEAS

It cannot be within the province of this book to convey more
than a fleeting glimpse of the state of public librarianship outside the United Kingdom. There is a growing interest in
international and comparative librarianship, and consequently
a growing literature, though still with many gaps. The United
States, for instance, being one of the countries which first
provided public libraries in the modern sense, will always be of
great interest, particularly for the many recent and remarkable
buildings provided. Cities such as Minneapolis, Seattle, New
Orleans and many others have main libraries worthy of the
closest study, while Washington, D.C. has recently opened a
huge main library of over 40,000 square metres in floor area.
The services provided by public libraries in the USA also merit
attention, particularly their audio-visual departments and their
services to young adults, to the physically handicapped, and to
that section of the community they refer to as the under-
privileged.

It may sometimes appear to librarians outside America that
the public library scene in the USA approaches the ideal, but
of course this is not the case. It is a big country, and coverage
is by no means so complete and uniform as it is in the United
Kingdom. Furthermore, our American colleagues have continuing budgetary problems and they have to contend with
potential censorship in a way that does not apply, at the time of
writing, in Scandinavia or the United Kingdom. Despite these
and other difficulties, public librarianship in the USA is in a
vital and interesting stage of development, and the student
should be aware of this. If a professional visit to the United
States cannot be made, something of the vitality of American
public librarians can be gained from a perusal of their periodicals such as *American Libraries*, *Library Journal* and the *Wilson
Bulletin*.

In Europe the most interesting area is undoubtedly Scandinavia where there is much to admire and learn. Once again

it is the public library buildings which attract, especially in Sweden, Finland and Denmark. Sweden has so many as to make a list impossible, except perhaps to say that Gothenburg's main library and branches are extremely worthy of study. Finland is one of the homes of contemporary architecture, and this is reflected in the public libraries at Kuopio, Rovaniemi and elsewhere. Denmark, too, has some striking buildings of recent origin at Randers and Lyngby-Tarbæk.

But it is in the co-operative field that Scandinavia excels. Each of the countries has set up library service agencies which centralize and can more cheaply carry out such processes as binding and cataloguing, as well as the production of standard stationery, bibliographies and booklists.

Similar agencies are at work in other European countries, especially in West Germany and Holland. Here it should be remarked that public library development in these two areas is now being carried out at an accelerated rate. In Belgium and France progress has not been so noticeable, but there are signs of life, and it would not be surprising if France soon became one of the leaders in public library progress.

There are public libraries in the Socialist countries too, and good examples may be seen in the Soviet Union, Poland, Romania, Hungary, Czechoslovakia and elsewhere. Direction is from a department of a Government ministry, which is often, as in Hungary, responsible for centralizing the methodology for public libraries. There are also trade union libraries which form an important feature of provision in the Socialist countries, and this necessitates close co-operation between the public and the trade union libraries.

Many developing countries have started public library services, with the assistance of unesco, the British Council and other agencies. The public library concept has in this way been started in India, Ceylon, the West Indies, and many of the newer states in the continents of Africa and Asia. Much has still to be done in these countries, but it is most encouraging to realize that the groundwork has been laid.

Chapter 3
How libraries are governed and financed

Student librarians should know at an early stage in their learning something of the authorities under which the various types of library are controlled, and the sources and means of their financial provision. This chapter endeavours to supply outline information on both these factors, but it is not an easy task since there are so many different kinds of libraries in existence today. Because public libraries employ more personnel than any other single type of library, the government and finance of public libraries will be described. But because the committee and financial structure of local authorities are broadly similar to those in the civil service, the universities and other concerns, student librarians aiming for these latter libraries need not think they are wasting their time by reading this chapter. In any case, brief notes are appended on the government and finance of special libraries, and those of the universities and Government departments.

Experience has shown that few aspirant librarians have any detailed knowledge of the constitution, powers and duties of local authority committees. Many student librarians, for instance, appear to labour under the delusion that libraries run themselves, or that their chief librarians are their sole arbiters. In addition to theoretical knowledge of this subject, students should try to acquire some practical experience of the workings of committees, their agendas, procedures, decision-making and minutes, though this is not easily done. One or two enlightened authorities have, in the past, allowed students and younger members of staff to attend committee meetings as spectators, and it is a pity that this practice has not become more widespread. Much, however, can be learnt from attending committee meetings in spheres connected with off-duty activities, since there exists a fairly general accepted code for the conduct of meetings.

COMMITTEE GOVERNMENT OF PUBLIC LIBRARIES

There have been radical changes in recent years in the committee government of public libraries in the United Kingdom. Although the appointment of a library committee was never obligatory to local authorities, except in Scotland, most library authorities did in fact include a library committee as one of their standing committees. The exceptions were the county councils, most of which governed their libraries through subcommittees of their Education Committees. Before the passing of the Public Libraries and Museums Act of 1964, the Minister of Education was pressed to include a clause making it obligatory for all library authorities, including the county councils, to appoint library committees by statute. The Minister refused to do this, though in the debates which preceded the passing of the Act by Parliament he gave every encouragement to county councils to do precisely this.

As a result of this clear encouragement, a large majority of the county councils did set up independent library committees, and it began to look as though in a matter of time all the public library authorities in the United Kingdom would have library committees included in their standing committees.

Local government, however, was under scrutiny about this time, and in the late 1960s two Government reports, known as the Maud Report and the Mallaby Report, were issued. One of these dealt mainly with local government staffing and the other concerned itself with local government structure and methods, including committee structure. Many local authorities began to reform their committee structures on the lines suggested in the Mallaby Report, which advocated a streamlining of committees. Although the Library Association strongly urged that local authorities should retain library committees, with chief librarians having the status of chief officers, many library committees were dissolved, and library business transferred to committees with other responsibilities.

The effect of this has not been as serious as was once thought, because local authorities also acted upon other recommendations of the Maud and Mallaby Committees, one of which was that committees had been dealing with too much *minutiae*, and that more powers should be delegated to chief officers. Where more powers have been given to chief librarians, this means that there is less business of a routine nature for committees, which can now devote their attention to matters of policy, planning, and capital and revenue budgeting. This reform has been entirely beneficial, but difficulties have arisen in many authorities in deciding to which committees to allocate library affairs. Some local authorities have placed library matters under their Education Committees, others have linked them with other miscellaneous services under such umbrella titles as Amenities Committee, Leisure Activities Committee or General Services Committee.

In the majority of local authorities the chief librarian is still a chief officer, but a number of other authorities have grouped their services under various directors and as a consequence their chief librarians are subordinate to an overall director and do not have direct reporting to their councils. This is quite contrary to the advice of the Library Association. It is difficult to assess the effect of this, since experience is so far limited, and so much depends upon the personalities of the director and the chief librarian. It could happen that under directorates public libraries could get a large share of the local authority's finances, especially where capital programmes are concerned, but it is too early yet to be able to say this with any definite proof.

THE COMMITTEE IN PRACTICE

Let us now examine the practical working of committees. The committees of a local authority meet in cycles, and the frequency of these is determined by each individual council. The old county councils used generally to meet quarterly, whereas the old city and town councils met more frequently, perhaps as much as eight or ten times a year.

The clerk to the council is responsible for sending out the notices of the meetings, for preparing the agenda, and for recording the minutes. The chief librarian is responsible for initiating items for the agenda, often in consultation with his chairman. The chief librarian is also responsible for preparing periodical reports on the work of the library, and for any other reports he is asked to prepare or wishes to submit. These he will send to the department of his authority which is responsible for sending out the agenda and notice convening the meeting.

At the committee meeting itself, an officer of the clerk's department will be present to give guidance when necessary, and there will also be a committee clerk to record the minutes and decisions of the meeting. Representatives of the financial, architectural and engineering departments will also be present in advisory capacities. Correspondence of a formal character is undertaken on behalf of the committee by the clerk and chief executive; that of a routine nature is conducted by the chief librarian.

COMMITTEE AGENDA

The contents of committee agenda will naturally vary from meeting to meeting but many items appear regularly. These include the minutes of the previous meeting, which after approval are signed by the chairman as a correct record. Accounts are also sometimes listed for approval, though many committees now leave financial arrangements within the approved budget in the hands of the professionals. The librarian's report is also a frequent item, but here again the tendency is to make this an annual, semi-annual or quarterly matter.

Some librarians are content to make their reports a bare tabulation of statistics, but efforts should be made to give reports a different news value. Without making the report too lengthy or tiresome, short paragraphs may be included to draw attention to library activities. Staff matters are usually the concern of the Establishment Committee, but if they are not, then they must be drawn to the attention of the committee responsible for libraries.

Such, then, are some of the regular items on committee agenda. Many other items, of course, crop up from time to time, such as suggested variations of opening hours, major alterations to buildings, plans for new or replacement libraries, or capital and revenue budgets. Most major items will be the subject of separate reports by the librarian, who must be expert in the art of report-writing. First it should be remembered that reports should be as brief as possible since committee members are busy people and have many reports to read. Paragraphs should be kept short and should be numbered consecutively for ease of reference. Every report should have a brief title and should carry an identifying number. In planning the report the librarian should endeavour to anticipate all possible questions and try to answer them in the report. Finally, if appropriate, the report should end with a clear recommendation or recommendations to the committee.

CONDUCT OF MEETINGS

The chairman of the committee responsible for libraries is a key person with whom the librarian should work in the closest co-operation. Items of major policy should be discussed with the chairman before they appear on the agenda. In order that the meeting may proceed expeditiously, and so that he shall have the fullest information on all topics on the agenda, the chairman is often provided with an annotated agenda. This is a private copy for the chairman, on which the librarian has subscribed explanatory notes and possible answers to anticipated questions from members of the committee. Alternatively, the chairman may have a conference before the meeting with the librarian and other advisory officers. At this briefing conference the chairman goes through the agenda with his officers, and he then has the opportunity to ask detailed questions, the answers to which undoubtedly help him in running the subsequent committee meeting.

The meeting of the committee is conducted by the chairman, and the librarian should generally speak only when he is invited to do so. But the officer is, after all, the professional adviser to the committee and the council, and all sensible chairmen and committees encourage, welcome and value his contributions to the meeting. For this reason the librarian should attend the meeting armed with all possible facts and figures relevant to the agenda. The meeting of the full council of a local authority is different; it is a meeting of elected members and, although chief officers including the librarian are present, only rarely are they consulted or requested to make a statement. For this reason, it is all the more important that the chairman should be kept fully informed, so that he can reply effectively to any points on library matters raised by the members of the council.

BUDGETS

Budgets are of two kinds – capital and revenue. Every local authority has a capital budget which it reviews annually, and such budgets are on a rolling programme, anticipating capital spending for five or sometimes even ten years ahead. Libraries usually are only concerned in the capital programme in relation to new library buildings or major alterations to existing ones. The wise librarian will therefore constantly be looking ahead and, in consultation with the finance and planning officers, will try not to miss any opportunities for including possible new buildings in the capital programme of his authority. Many local authorities are now making use of programme planned budgeting systems (PPBS), so this is one more development which librarians must learn about, and in which they must participate. In PPBS it is necessary first to define objectives, so the librarian must be ready to do this, remembering to include all aspects of the library service and its ancillaries.

The revenue budget is the one which is considered annually, first by the committee responsible for libraries, then by the finance committee, and finally by the council. The revenue budget, or annual estimates, are prepared for the committee by the finance department, but in consultation with the librarian and other chief officers concerned. The librarian, therefore, has to be prepared at an early stage to state his requirements. When these involve special works, repairs and maintenance, and new furniture and equipment, estimates have to be obtained from the appropriate sources before they can be included in the following year's budget.

There is a simple and fairly standard form of presentation, as follows.

EXPENDITURE

Item	Estimated expenditure 1973–74 £	Actual expenditure 1973–74 £	Estimated expenditure 1974–75 £
Salaries and wages	400,000	403,870	450,000
Books	200,000	200,000	225,000
Binding	25,000	25,000	28,000
Periodicals	18,000	18,500	20,000
Printing and stationery	7,000	7,000	7,200
Gas, electricity and fuel	8,500	8,200	8,600
Rents and rates	13,000	13,000	14,000
Loan charges	28,000	28,000	28,000
etc. etc.			

INCOME

Item	Estimated income 1973–74 £	Actual income 1973–74 £	Estimated income 1974–75 £
Charges for overdue books	12,000	12,250	13,000
Reservations of books	8,000	8,250	9,000
Lost and damaged books	500	500	500
Rents	2,450	2,450	2,600
Sale of catalogues, publications	2,100	1,975	2,000
Hire of halls	1,500	1,675	1,750
etc. etc.			

The above figures are, of course, hypothetical, and should not be regarded as actual or proportionate for any particular public library system. It is sometimes the custom for the income and expenditure of each branch library to be itemized separately, so that the running costs of each one can be seen, but where possible finance officers prefer to collect all the figures together, and there is no doubt that this makes it easier for the budget to be understood by committee and council members.

After the budget has been thus drafted, it is duplicated and printed, and copies are sent to committee members prior to the meeting which will consider it. At the meeting, each item will be scrutinized and the librarian may be called upon to explain and justify his financial requirements for the coming year. Since the book fund is one of the major items, the librarian will obviously be well prepared to justify any increase he is seeking. Other questions may concern the break-down of such omnibus items as 'Furniture and equipment', 'Printing, stationery and advertising', 'Alterations and special works', 'Conferences and travel expenses' and 'Repairs and maintenance', and the librarian should have the necessary memoranda with him to answer such questions in detail.

When the budget has been fully considered and finally approved, it is then transmitted to the Finance Committee, which usually considers the budgets of all committees of the local authority at a specially convened meeting or meetings. A Finance Committee sometimes has the power to alter budgets of other committees, but more often if it has any observations to make on the budget of another committee it refers this back for further consideration of some items. It sometimes goes further and gives some indication of the amount of the variations which it considers necessary.

After the budget has been approved by the Finance Committee, the figures are sent to the council of the authority for final consideration and approval, and it then becomes the official budget for the ensuing year. For his own department, the librarian is the officer responsible for keeping items of expenditure within the approved budget, especially in such direct items of expenditure as books, gramophone records, microtexts, binding, printing, furniture and equipment. Under some headings, such as salaries and wages, electricity or postages, overspendings are often outside the librarian's control, due perhaps to unexpected salary awards or unanticipated rises in postage rates or electricity charges.

SUPPLEMENTARY ESTIMATES

The financial year for local authorities in England and Wales runs usually from April 1 of one year to March 31 of the next, and the annual budget covers income and expenditure over that period. Sometimes circumstances arise which necessitate urgent consideration of extra expenditure in the middle of the financial year. When this happens, the librarian places the facts before his committee and requests what is known as a supplementary estimate. This, after approval by the committee responsible for libraries, is forwarded to the Finance Committee, and if it meets with approval there, it goes to the council for ultimate consideration and sanction. In normal circumstances, the librarian and his committee should make every effort to avoid asking for supplementary estimates, which are naturally not popular with finance committees.

An effort has been made in the foregoing to give an account of the committee responsible for libraries at work, but it is difficult to describe practical committee work in the pages of a book. What has been described is fairly general practice in local authorities, but there are of course differences in detail from one authority to another. Aspirant librarians should endeavour first to acquire some knowledge of how their own libraries are governed and financed, and then go on to compare this with the practices of other library authorities or other types of library.

GOVERNMENT OF NATIONAL, ACADEMIC AND SPECIAL LIBRARIES

As we have seen in chapter 1 there are many libraries which are financed wholly from central Government funds. In addition to the British Library and other national collections, there are the libraries of Government departments such as the Department of Trade and Industry. All these come under one or other of the Whitehall ministries, so that Parliament is the body which ultimately controls them, and Ministers of the Crown are responsible to Parliament for their administration and management. As far as their finances are concerned, they are organized in a way very similar to the local authority libraries, because they work on a year-to-year basis, preparing budgets for coming years, and these have to be considered at departmental level and by the Treasury before final approval by Parliament.

University libraries in the United Kingdom are governed by library committees of the universities. At Cambridge, the members of the committee are known as Syndics, while at Oxford they are called Curators. At the other universities the library committee consists of professors and lecturers, and there is usually no limit to the size of such committees, although the average membership is from twelve to twenty members. In Scotland the university library committee is composed of representatives from the non-university governing body. As for the financing of a university library, it will no doubt be known that there is a body known as the University Grants Committee which calls for budgets on a five-yearly basis for the running of the whole of every university, including the library. In spite of this, the university is run on a year-to-year basis, on estimates culled from the five-year budgetary programme. Some of the older universities have some endowments for their libraries, but the income from these is now nowhere near enough to run them, and the Treasury grants through the UGC help to bridge the gaps.

It may well be imagined that in a university, which by very reason of its name, endeavours to instruct in a wide range of subjects, there could well be keen competition by the various faculties, institutes and departments for representation of their subjects in the university library. To control this, and to secure equitable treatment, there are sometimes set up book selection committees, so that additions to the library can be fairly allocated.

It is difficult to generalize about the government and financing of special libraries, since they fall into a number of different categories. There are special libraries owned by bodies such as the National Book League, and many belonging to professional associations such as the Royal Society of Medicine, the Royal Institute of British Architects or the Library Association. Libraries of this kind are almost always governed by specially appointed committees, are financed out of the general subscription income from members, and they work on an annual budget basis.

But we must not forget the many special libraries which belong to industrial organizations such as ICI, Boots, Kodak or the Metal Box Company. An increasing number of these industrial libraries have chartered librarians in charge, with specialist staffs to help them, and they too are organized on a yearly financial basis. The overriding authority for the government and financing of this kind of special library will, of course, be the board of directors of the firm.

COMPARATIVE LIBRARY GOVERNMENT

Brief reference must be made to what happens in other countries. In general, what has been described above as United Kingdom practice for national, academic and special libraries applies also in most advanced library countries. But there are important differences abroad as far as public libraries are concerned. In the United States and Scandinavia, to mention only two areas, the public library is governed by a board which is outside the purview of the city or county council. When a major new library building is mooted in the United States, this has to be voted by a majority of the residents at an election, and capital is raised by a bond issue. These practices necessitate a much more positive public relations programme than most British public libraries have ever indulged in. The board of a public library in the United States or Scandinavia is usually much smaller in number than a British committee, being rarely larger than seven and sometimes having only five members. It also meets more infrequently, since the director or chief librarian has wide executive powers and the board concerns itself only with matters of major policy. As we have seen earlier, this trend is now spreading rapidly in the United Kingdom, and not before it was time.

The financing of public libraries outside the United Kingdom often involves state aid, though the lion's share of library income still comes from the local authorities from the local tax income. State aid has been a special feature of Scandinavian public libraries: it was brought about mainly because the communities in such countries as Norway and Sweden are small and scattered, and many were obviously not viable enough to maintain public libraries at the desired level of service.

The board system of governing libraries in the United States has advantages and disadvantages compared with the committee government common in the United Kingdom. American librarians have been heard to express preference for the British system, while British librarians have at the same time admired the American idea. After the aspirant librarian has taken his first steps in librarianship he may sometimes be spurred to investigate this problem further by making deeper comparisons between the American and the British traditions of public library government.

Chapter 4
Co-operation between libraries

Co-operation between libraries began as the approach to an ideal, that of being able to supply any book or written information for any reader anywhere. At one time, if a reader entered his library and asked for a book which was not in the stock of that library he was told that the book was not available and had to go away unsatisfied. Sometimes the library would take a request and order the book specially, but more often than not the book was out-of-print and unobtainable.

Now, thanks to the many schemes of library co-operation which have been built up in the last fifty years, it can be said with some certainty that when a reader enters his own library he virtually enters at the same time the doors of nearly every other library in the country, and quite a number outside the country, since co-operation has now been developed on international as well as national lines.

In the succeeding sections of this chapter a modicum of historical information relating to the growth of library co-operation will be afforded to the student, but within the compass of this book there is no space to dwell in detail upon the complete history of library co-operation in the United Kingdom and elsewhere. For this, the reader is directed to other sources, of which there are many.

THE NATIONAL CENTRAL LIBRARY

The idea of library co-operation was mooted several times by different people in the late nineteenth and early twentieth centuries. Sidney Webb (later Lord Passfield) suggested co-operation between London's public libraries in 1904, but it was a quarter of a century later before this began to happen. The first step in library co-operation in the United Kingdom was taken in 1915 when Professor W. G. S. Adams, in a *Report on Library Provision and Policy* made to the Carnegie United Kingdom Trustees, suggested that a central lending library for adult education classes would be of great use. As a result of this, the Central Library for Students was formed in 1916 chiefly to supply books to adult classes such as those of the Workers' Educational Association.

The need for such a library was soon apparent from the measure of the work it accomplished and, thanks to the financial support of the Carnegie United Kingdom Trust, it developed rapidly in scope and use. In 1927 the Kenyon Report recommended that the library should be reconstituted as a national central lending library and that it should be based on the British Museum. The Trustees of the British Museum were unable to concur with this suggestion, and they proposed instead that the Central Library for Students should become an independent national institution with its own board of trustees.

The Government of the day referred the matter to the Royal Commission on National Museums and Galleries, which was sitting at the time, and after taking evidence the Commission suggested that the Central Library should reconstitute itself under its own board of trustees and that a grant-in-aid should be made by the Exchequer. In 1930 this took place and the Central Library for Students became the National Central Library. A Royal Charter followed in 1931.

At that time the NCL lent many books to public libraries and the Trustees were urged by the Royal Commission to try to increase their income from local authorities. Some success resulted from the ensuing appeals, and with the Rockefeller Foundation and the CUKT grants added to the Treasury grant and the subscriptions from user libraries, the financial position of the NCL slowly improved. From 1930 onwards the regional library systems were formed and these, as well as relieving the NCL of a heavy load of interlibrary loans, gave added ensured income as the public libraries contributed through their regional library systems. In addition, more non-public libraries saw the value of the NCL and their subscriptions, however modest, were always welcome and helpful.

The library, which was originally housed in Tavistock Square and later in Galen Place, moved to Malet Place in 1933 into a building generously supplied by the CUKT. Unfortunately it had a severe setback during the 1939–45 war when it was damaged by air raids and lost about 100,000 books. The work of reconstructing the building was finished in 1952, largely from funds provided by the War Damage Commission, but also with valued financial help from the CUKT. Since 1965 the NCL has been housed in a new building in Store Street, and since 1962 it has had the use of some Government premises at Woolwich as a deposit library for reserve stock. The work of replenishing the book stock has been a slow process but the present figure has reached 650,000 volumes.

Over the years the character of the stock of the NCL has changed several times. After the advent of the regional library systems, and more so since the beginning of the various schemes of subject specialization, the library began to act more as a clearing house for the organization of interlibrary loans and for the supply of bibliographical information. It was never completely reliant upon its own stock because, even before the start of the regional schemes, it had organized a system of Outlier Libraries. These were a number of public, academic and special libraries throughout the United Kingdom which agreed to lend books to other libraries through the agency of the NCL. The Outlier Libraries, which reached at peak a total of more than 400, were all specialist institutions and between them they loaned more than 26,000 volumes annually, a notable contribution to the machinery of library co-operation.

A union catalogue is a list, showing locations, of the stock of any number of libraries in an organized area. Within the NCL there have been a number of union catalogues, the two major ones being the National Union Catalogue which is in sheaf form and covers the stocks of the libraries in the regional schemes, and the Outlier Union Catalogue which is in card form and includes the holdings of many special, university and college libraries. Unfortunately, both union catalogues fell into arrears owing to shortages of staff and funds, and although this did not prevent them from being valuable tools, they were obviously not as useful as they would have been if complete.

The profession as a whole was deeply concerned about the union catalogue arrears and in the 1950s the Vollans Report and the Roberts Report, as well as the Working Party Report

of 1962 entitled *Inter-Library Co-operation in England and Wales*,
all suggested that urgent attention should be given to clearing
the arrears of work. Some progress has been made in this
direction. Meanwhile, as a result of an inter-regional coverage
scheme for current British books which has been in operation
since 1959, and to which later reference will be made (see p. 62),
the character of the book stock of the NCL has again changed.
As a result of the existence of this scheme, the library has been
able to concentrate on adding a greater number of foreign,
especially American, material.

The NCL, the regions, and the Outlier Libraries have operated
as follows. University and special libraries apply directly to the
NCL, but public libraries generally apply first to their region.
Requests which cannot be supplied from within the region are
then sent on to the NCL. In the first place the NCL endeavours to
satisfy the request from its own stock, but if this is impossible it
then tries to locate a copy in its union catalogues. Only about
one-fifth of all satisfied requests are met from the stock of the
NCL itself, with university libraries meeting about 40 per cent,
public libraries about 20 per cent, and the Outlier and other
libraries the remaining 20 per cent. When a holding library
receives a request from another library via the NCL it sends the
book directly to the borrowing library.

Mention must be made of the growth of international library
co-operation, which has been largely fostered by the NCL. If
a book requested is not available in any United Kingdom
library, foreign libraries are contacted by the NCL and an international library loan is frequently made through its agency. In
1970–71, 6,176 volumes were borrowed in this way for British
readers, the majority of the books coming from West Germany,
France, East Germany, the USSR, and Italy. Loans by British
libraries through the NCL to foreign libraries have been made
at the rate of about 5,600 a year, so that the system is two-way.

One of the functions of the NCL as set out in its Royal Charter
is to act as a centre of bibliographical information, both
national and international, and several activities are designed
to further this object. There is a Bureau of American Bibliography, a Union Catalogue of Russian books and periodicals,
and a Union Catalogue of German wartime books and periodicals. In addition the NCL maintains a growing collection of

bibliographies which it draws upon in the operation of its bibliographic enquiry service.

Other activities of the NCL include the *British Union Catalogue of Periodicals* (BUCOP) which since 1962 it has kept up-to-date and issued cumulated volumes. It also operates the British National Book Centre, which since 1948 has arranged the re-distribution of redundant material. If a member library has books or journals for withdrawal, it can offer them to other potentially interested libraries before withdrawing them. Lists are sent to the BNBC which collates all the titles it receives and circulates the master-list at intervals to all the member libraries for checking. In this way about 100,000 items per annum are redistributed, and since its inception BNBC has helped to relocate well over two million items.

The NCL has been on telex for a number of years, by which means it contacts directly the regions, the NLL, and many university, public and Outlier libraries which also use telex. It also has a photocopying service which helps to speed up the supply of specific requests. Finally, the NCL continues its adult class work which was, so to speak, the fount of its existence. This lending of multiple copies of set books to adult classes is, however, gradually declining, owing to the fact that the larger public library systems of today are able to take over more of this work.

As we have seen in chapter 1, the NCL is to become part of the British Library and its main operations are being transferred to Boston Spa as part of the extended National Lending Library. It has not yet been decided what use will be made of the present NCL building in Store Street, London.

THE REGIONAL LIBRARY SYSTEMS

As we know them today, the regional library systems date generally from the 1930s, although there were tentative schemes in operation before then. There are, at the time of writing, ten separate schemes covering England, Wales and Scotland. The earliest to be formed was the London Union Catalogue (LUC), founded in 1929 with the assistance of a grant from the CUKT and taken over by the Metropolitan Boroughs

Standing Joint Committee in 1934. It was housed in the NCL and its union catalogue served the old twenty-eight metropolitan boroughs and the City of London. It was the base on which the London public libraries erected a notable edifice of library co-operation. Apart from satisfying over 40,000 requests annually, the LUC arranged for complete interavailability of public library use within its area, devised the Metropolitan Special Collections (MSC) scheme of subject specialization, provided a Metropolitan Joint Fiction Reserve (MJFR), and devised a scheme within its member libraries for foreign fiction specialization. It also inaugurated a union catalogue of play sets and a union list of annuals and periodicals taken by the libraries in its membership.

The past tense is used because in 1969 the LUC was merged with the South Eastern Regional Library System (SERLS) to become the London and South Eastern Region (LASER).

Following the lead given by London, in 1931 three regional library systems were inaugurated, those of Wales and Monmouthshire, the Northern, and the West Midlands. The Welsh schemes were based on Cardiff and Aberystwyth, the former covering Glamorgan and Monmouthshire, and the latter covering the remainder of Wales. Both have union catalogues and since 1953 there has been a subject specialization scheme in operation. Between them the two systems serve seventy-five libraries, including special and university libraries. In 1972 the decision was taken to amalgamate the two Welsh union catalogues. The Northern Regional Library System, with headquarters at Newcastle upon Tyne serves seventy-six libraries in Cumberland, Durham, Northumberland, Westmorland and a part of Yorkshire. It has a union catalogue and handles about 20,000 requests each year. The West Midlands Regional Library System is housed at the Birmingham Central Library and has a membership of eighty-five, including college, university and special as well as public libraries. The counties covered are Herefordshire, Shropshire, Staffordshire, Warwickshire and Worcestershire, and about 27,000 requests are handled annually.

In 1933 the South Eastern Regional Library System was formed, and had its headquarters at the NCL. Covering the counties of Bedfordshire, Berkshire, Buckinghamshire, Essex,

Hertfordshire, Kent, Middlesex, Surrey and Sussex it served a larger population than any other system. A subject specialization scheme, based on BNB entries, operated from 1950. As we have seen, the SERLS voluntarily merged with the LUC in 1969 to form LASER, now by far the largest regional library system and covering the whole of Greater London as well as the nine counties mentioned above. It thus serves a population of nearly seventeen million and has access to book stocks of thirty million volumes. It is handling over 160,000 applications yearly and its resources, helped by the London and Home Counties Branch of the LA, have already enabled it to introduce the technique of Computer Output Microfilm for its union catalogue. One subject specialization scheme is being maintained under the auspices of LASER, and this is the one based on the MSC collections of the Inner London boroughs.

The East Midlands and the North Western Regional Library Systems both date from 1935. The former is housed at the Leicester City Library and serves a population of over eight million in nine different counties. It has a membership of seventy-three libraries and handles over 30,000 requests every year. It recently took part in an experiment involving closer collaboration with the NCL. The North Western System is housed at Manchester City Library and serves seven million people in Lancashire, Cheshire and the Isle of Man. No fewer than 110 libraries are in membership, including thirty-three academic and special libraries. Over 40,000 requests are received annually and since 1954 a subject specialization scheme has been operated.

Also dating from 1935 is the Yorkshire Regional Library System, housed at Sheffield and dealing with 16,000 requests every year from fifty institutional members. A feature of the Yorkshire system is that there is no union catalogue as the scheme works through Zonal and Sub-zonal centres, and normally only eighteen libraries are asked to lend through the system.

The South Western Regional Library System was formed in 1937, and although it was the last to appear it is only fair to add that it incorporated the Cornwall scheme which had been working since 1927. It has a membership of eighty-nine libraries of all types in Cornwall, Devon, Dorset, Gloucestershire,

Hampshire, the Isle of Wight, Oxfordshire, Somerset and Wiltshire. Its headquarters is at Bristol and it handles over 35,000 applications every year with the help of a union catalogue.

In Scotland there is a counterpart to the NCL in the shape of the Scottish Central Library (SCL) which was founded in 1921, thanks once again to the CUKT. It was not until 1939 that the decision was taken to form a regional library system for Scotland and owing to the war it was not begun until 1945. Known as the Scottish Union Catalogue, it has about 150 member libraries of all types. It handles over 20,000 requests each year and since 1955 has operated a joint reserve of the works of Scottish novelists.

Over the years there have been numerous calls for the rationalization of the regions on the grounds that there are too many of them. The Minister of Education's Working Party on *Inter-Library Co-operation in England and Wales* reported in 1962 and recommended this, and the Public Libraries and Museums Act of 1964 requires the Secretary of State to designate areas as library regions in England and Wales and to make schemes for such regions. Up to now, only one change has ensued, and that was the merger of LUC and SERLS to form LASER. The reason why the other regions have so far been left as they were is because the Secretary of State for Education and Science is awaiting the changes which will accrue from local government reorganization. There is little doubt that there will soon be other combinations of existing regions, and there may eventually be no more than four or five regional library systems in the country.

SUBJECT SPECIALIZATION

The term 'subject specialization' has already been frequently used, and some explanation of it is overdue. It is really another name for co-operative bookbuying and it became necessary when it was found that in most schemes of library co-operation libraries were tending to duplicate their book selection. As a result there were perhaps too many copies in regions of certain books, and not enough copies of other titles. The libraries of the old metropolitan London were the first to begin a comprehensive scheme, which they did in 1948, each library agreeing to spend a minimum sum on the subjects allocated to it. Additionally, they agreed to include periodicals and foreign books on the subjects in which they were specializing, and also to store and preserve their acquisitions on these subjects.

As we have seen, this subject specialization scheme has become the base for the special collections of LASER. Meanwhile, other schemes of subject specialization have been operating for some years in Wales, the East Midlands, the North Western and other regions.

It will already have been appreciated that the regional library systems were set up independently of each other, and that their constitutions, routines and services vary considerably. However great these divergences may be, they would have been still wider had it not been for the existence, since 1931, of a body called the National Committee for Regional Library Co-operation (NCRLC). This committee, consisting of representatives from the regions, the NCL, the LA, the CUKT, and the universities, has attempted to co-ordinate all the co-operative schemes in the country and has had a beneficial effect on them.

As well as standardizing the application form used by the NCL and the regions, the NCRLC evolved an inter-regional coverage scheme for British current books since January 1, 1959. This extended the idea of subject specialization from individual regions to the nation as a whole, and enabled inter-library loans of post-1958 British material recorded in BNB to be arranged directly between the regions concerned. This relieved the NCL of considerable responsibility and enabled it to spend more of its scanty funds on older books and on foreign, and especially American, books. The NCRLC also evolved a National Joint Fiction Reserve covering the whole of England except London and the South East, which has its own scheme.

Details of each region's commitments under these schemes are as follows:

East Midlands:	DC classes 400 and 800. Fiction authors G–J.
LASER	DC class 700.
Northern:	DC class 000. Fiction authors D–F.
North Western:	DC class 600. Fiction authors A–C.
Scotland:	DC classes 350–399.
South Western:	DC class 200. Fiction authors T–Z.

Wales and
  Monmouthshire: DC class 100.
West Midlands: DC class 500. Fiction authors K–M.
Yorkshire: DC classes 300–349. Fiction authors N–S.

It should be noted that replacement of the NCRLC by a joint committee appointed by the Advisory Councils for England and Wales was envisaged in the Public Libraries and Museums Act of 1964, but this has been held up by local government re-organization and final decisions on the mergers between the existing regions.

NATIONAL LENDING LIBRARY FOR SCIENCE AND TECHNOLOGY

Considerable reference has already been made to the National Lending Library for Science and Technology, which for some years operated as the DSIR Lending Library Unit auxiliary to the Science Museum Library. In 1962 however, the NLL, as it is briefly referred to, began to occupy a site at Boston Spa in Yorkshire and was officially opened in November of that year. The main purpose of the library is 'to supplement the internal resources of existing organizations by providing a rapid loan service'. Some of the Science Library's stock was transferred to the NLL and this was supplemented from other sources. Although many books are included in the NLL, it has relied mainly on its vast and increasing holdings of scientific and technical periodicals culled from all over the world. In recent years it has widened its area to include the social sciences.

The NLL has been described as a 'practitioner's library', and it has cut down its records to the absolute minimum. Much microform material is held, and photocopies of articles from journals or chapters from books can be and are promptly supplied. Both book and periodical holdings are arranged by title, and use is made of conveyor belts, photocopiers and any sophisticated hardware that will aid the rapid provision of material for users. The library is on telex and its lending is organized through other libraries of all types. In less than ten years it became a vital and unique link in the chain of British library co-operation.

Although co-operation between libraries has been developed probably more in Britain than in any other country, and indeed it has been the admiration and envy of many other countries, British librarians have never been satisfied and have been seeking to improve and rationalize it for many years. In the 1950s the Vollans Report and the Roberts Report both made recommendations, some of which have been implemented, but it was not until after the appearance of the Dainton Committee Report in 1969 that drastic reorganization was put on the drawing-board. Most of the Dainton Report recommendations were accepted by the Government in its White Paper *The British Library* (Cmnd. 4572) issued in 1971.

The Dainton Report dealt in some detail with the NLL and the NCL, recommending that the loan stocks of the NCL should be transferred to Boston Spa. As has been seen, the Government has incorporated both the NLL and the NCL into the British Library, and this complex of lending services is in fact being transferred to Boston Spa. When this transfer has taken place, and when rationalization of the library regions is completed, Britain should have a system of library co-operation second to none in the world.

SPECIALIST SCHEMES OF CO-OPERATION

One of the failings of library co-operation in the 1930s, based as it was on the NCL and the infant regional systems, was that it did little for specialists. The requirements of industry and technology, the needs of legal and medical students, the demands for music and play sets, and the multifarious enquiries from business and commerce, all combined to help in inaugurating a number of *ad hoc* co-operative systems.

The earliest of these was the Sheffield Interchange Organization (SINTO) which was mooted in 1932 and began to operate a year later. In this scheme, special libraries in the Sheffield area joined together to make their book and periodical holdings mutually available through the agency of the science and commerce department of Sheffield City Libraries. After 1945 the Sheffield lead was followed in many areas such as West London, Tyneside, Manchester, Liverpool, Hertfordshire,

Nottingham and Leicester. There are now over thirty such schemes in being, rejoicing in acronyms like HERTIS (Hertford-shire Technical Information Service) and TALIC (Tyneside Association of Libraries for Industry and Commerce).

Academic and special libraries are not being left behind in this direction and SCONUL has worked out several co-operative projects for its members, while SCOTAPLL (Standing Conference of Theological and Philosophical Libraries in London) has published a directory and a union list of periodicals, as well as having initiated an interavailability scheme.

In the past legal and medical students have been an embar-rassment to public libraries because of their demands for the latest editions of textbooks, but most public libraries now subscribe to Lewis's Medical and Scientific Library and to the Law Notes Lending Library, both of which issue printed catalogues of their stocks. The London Library, rich in nineteenth-century books, has a similar plan whereby other libraries may borrow from its stocks on a subscription basis, and many progressive public libraries make use of this facility.

For music there is the Central Music Library which operates under the aegis of Westminster City Libraries. In a strict sense the name Central Music Library Ltd means the collection originally formed by Mrs Christie Moór, which was deposited with the Westminster City Council in 1947. Retaining its independent status and character, it is supplemented by the large and rapidly growing collections of the City Libraries' Music Division. The stock now consists of over 80,000 items, and loans are made through the national interlending schemes as well as personally at the library, which accepts current tickets from any library in the United Kingdom. The CML is housed at the Victoria Library, Buckingham Palace Road, London, SW1W 9UD.

The CML is not strong in orchestral sets, though it is building up stocks in this area. For the borrowing of orchestral sets, libraries usually apply to the Henry Watson Music Library, Manchester, loans being obtainable from this collection against a small annual subscription.

A more recent development in co-operation has taken place in relation to play sets. There is a large demand from schools, colleges and societies for the provision of acting editions of

5

plays in sets and this challenge has been taken up by numerous public libraries such as Luton, Plymouth and libraries in the counties and in the London boroughs, most of which have useful collections. It was inevitable that a pooling of resources should take place and now LASER and the East Midlands systems have schemes for the interlending of play sets, maintaining union lists of their stocks.

INTERAVAILABILITY OF LIBRARY USE

The successful operation of the regional systems helped considerably to break down the parish-pump attitude between local libraries, and nowadays there are many examples of the interavailability of use between library and library. Complete interavailability exists, for instance, between the libraries of the London boroughs, including the City of London, and also between the co-operating libraries of SCOTAPLL. Reciprocal agreements between neighbouring libraries abound all over the country. Holiday resorts have for many years accepted current library tickets from visitors, wherever their home libraries may be, and official encouragement has been given to public libraries in the United Kingdom to extend this privilege freely. One cannot yet say that readers' tickets may be proffered and used at any library in the country, but the reality is imminent.

LIBRARY CO-OPERATION IN OTHER COUNTRIES

British geography, so much a disadvantage where climate is concerned, has assisted the development of schemes of library co-operation because of the small and compact size of the country. Probably no other country in the world can approach Britain either in the progress made in library co-operation or in the use made of it. The United States, by virtue of its size, has no national scheme, although the Farmington Plan for university library co-operation is deservedly well known. There are also, in the United States, some effective and developed regional schemes of which the Mid-West Interlibrary Center in Chicago and the Pacific Northwest Bibliographic Center in

Seattle are just two examples. The latter is very interesting since as well as covering libraries in the American states of Idaho, Montana, Oregon and Washington, it includes the Canadian libraries in British Columbia. It has a union catalogue with locations, arranges interlibrary loans, encourages subject specialization and generally acts as a clearing house for regional co-operation between libraries.

The nearest approaches elsewhere to the British networks can be found in Scandinavia. Denmark, Norway and Sweden all have carefully worked-out schemes. In Denmark the State and University Library at Århus meets all requests for Danish books as it is a copyright library, and it supplies many foreign (non-Danish) books as well. To cope further with the many demands from Danish readers for foreign books there is an Information Office in Copenhagen which maintains a union catalogue of the foreign holdings of Danish libraries.

Denmark was also one of the first countries abroad to follow up the British idea of interavailability of library use, and many libraries in the area of Greater Copenhagen take part in a workable scheme of this kind.

One of the first concerns of any developing country which is embarking upon a nationally integrated library programme should certainly be to plan schemes of library co-operation from the outset, and not to build them up piecemeal. Co-operation is an essential element in any national library service, but it can only work properly when there is a carefully thought-out master-plan behind it.

Chapter 5
Library Associations

The last hundred years has witnessed a remarkable growth in librarianship as a profession, and it is not surprising to find that, in almost every country, librarians have organized themselves into general and specific associations. The countries which were first in the field of library development were, not unnaturally, also the first to form societies of librarians for the purpose of discussing mutual problems. The American Library Association, for instance, was inaugurated in 1876 and was followed, only a year later, by the Library Association in the United Kingdom. Now almost every country is similarly organized, and a fairly full list of library associations of the world may be found in the current *Library Association Year Book*. This useful list contains not only the name and address of each association, but also the name of its president and/or secretary, and its official publications.

INTERNATIONAL LIBRARY ASSOCIATIONS

Organizations of librarians have been formed not just nationally, but internationally as well. The major international body in the field is the International Federation of Library Associations, known as IFLA. This really began as an international committee in 1928, and it is only since 1953 that it has been constituted as the IFLA General Council. Although it is not so much an association of librarians as a collection of representatives from library associations, IFLA has obviously owed its progress to the dedicated work of many individual librarians all over the world. In recent years it has extended its membership and influence by permitting individual libraries and library schools to become affiliated members.

IFLA's governing body is its Executive Board which is small in number, but there is also a much wider based Consultative Committee. The more detailed work of the Federation is carried out by its sections and committees and, without listing all these, it should be mentioned that there are sections for national and university libraries, for public libraries, for special libraries and for parliamentary and administrative libraries. There are also subsections concerned with libraries in hospitals, work with children, astronomical and geographical libraries, as well as committees with work relating to library education, library buildings, statistics, periodicals, rare books and many other aspects of the profession. Another body operating under the umbrella of IFLA is the International Association of Metropolitan City Libraries (INTAMEL), the name of which is sufficient indication of the range and scope of its activities. INTAMEL is engaged on many research study projects relating to the common problems of metropolitan city library administration, and it arranges a working party meeting once a year.

IFLA's General Council also meets once a year, first in one country, then another, and a very full programme is arranged. The present headquarters of the permanent secretariat of IFLA is at The Hague, Holland. Publications of IFLA include the periodical *Libri*, as well as the *IFLA Annual*.

Since 1945 the United Nations has played a prominent part in international librarianship through UNESCO, the United Nations Educational, Scientific and Cultural Organization. Rather than acting as a link between the world's library associations as IFLA does, UNESCO has concerned itself more with the task of spreading the public library concept throughout the world. It is reasonable to say that before 1939 the public library idea had developed only in the United States, in the United Kingdom and the Commonwealth, and in the Scandinavian countries. It has been the task of UNESCO, working from its Paris headquarters, to introduce libraries to those countries which have not had the benefit of them, and to foster their development.

To this end it has organized pilot library projects in India, Ghana, Nigeria, Colombia and other countries. Neither has UNESCO's work for international librarianship ended here. It has in addition encouraged and assisted the international exchange of publications, made major contributions to international bibliography, set up its own library and information office, and published much valuable material, including the well-known *Unesco Bulletin for Libraries*, which appears six times a year.

There are several other international associations of note, including the International Association of Music Libraries (IAML) and the International Association of Technological University Libraries (IATUL). The former has a United Kingdom branch which organizes meetings and publishes occasional bulletins. The IAML itself issues the journal *Fontes Artis Musicae* three times yearly.

THE LIBRARY ASSOCIATION

In the United Kingdom the oldest and the largest organization of librarians is the Library Association, which was founded in 1877 and granted its Royal Charter in 1898. At the outset scholarly librarians took much of the initiative and formed the majority of the membership, but as the urban libraries grew in number in the 1880s and 1890s, the number and influence of public librarians in the Association increased accordingly. This newer type of librarian grew impatient of the antiquarian bias of the scholarly members and wanted more discussion of the problems of the growing public libraries. Gradually the emphasis of the Library Association changed and it became more concerned with the promotion of public libraries, although in theory it still retained its interest in the development of libraries in general, as the Royal Charter of 1898 plainly demonstrates. The purpose and powers of the Association, as outlined in the Charter, are as follows:

(1) To unite all persons engaged or interested in library work, by holding conferences and meetings for the discussion of bibliographical questions and matters affecting libraries or their regulation or management or otherwise.

(2) To promote the better administration of Libraries.

(3) To promote whatever may tend to the improvement of the position and the qualifications of Librarians.

(4) To promote the adoption of the Public Libraries Acts in any City, Borough or other district within the United Kingdom of Great Britain and Ireland.

(5) To promote the establishment of reference and lending Libraries for use by the public.

(6) To watch any legislation affecting Public Libraries, and to assist in the promotion of such further legislation as may be considered necessary for the regulation and management or extension of Public Libraries.

(7) To promote and encourage bibliographical study and research.

(8) To collect, collate, and publish (in the form of Transactions, Journals, or otherwise) information of service or interest to the Fellows and Members of the Association, or for the promotion of the objects of the Corporation.

(9) To form, collect, and maintain a Library and Museum.

(10) To hold examinations in Librarianship and to issue Certificates of efficiency.

(11) To do all such lawful things as are incidental or conducive to the attainment of the above objects.

Since the dawn of the present century libraries have developed in many directions and there is no doubt that the Library Association, dominated as it was by public librarians, was slow to recognize the changes and as a consequence missed many opportunities. If it had been otherwise, such bodies as Aslib (Association of Special Libraries and Information Bureaux) and the School Library Association may never have been brought into existence. Nevertheless, it is easy to criticize after the event, and the pattern of the Library Association's progress has followed, admittedly at several removes, the historical sequence of library development generally.

After the formation of Aslib in 1924, the Library Association woke up to the fact that new types of libraries were creating fresh problems and new personnel who could not be satisfied with a purely public library approach. In 1929 revised byelaws came into force allowing for the formation of sections, although in fact the County Libraries Section and the University and Research Libraries Section were already in existence. Soon after the Second World War the Youth Libraries Section was formed, and this was rapidly followed by the Medical Section and the Reference and Special Libraries Section. Parallel with these sections is the Association of Assistant Librarians, founded in 1895, but which became a section of the Library Association in 1930.

Although this organization was not perfect, it was a great improvement on what it had been thirty years previously, and the improvement was reflected in the Library Association's membership, which was 240 in 1880, 2,800 in 1930 and 15,000 in 1963. Membership at the time of writing (1972) is over 21,000.

In 1961 the Library Association underwent a radical internal reorganization, transforming it into a truly professional body. The sections became known as groups, though four of them retain the old terminology of 'Section', only personal members could vote at the annual or special general meetings, and the committee structure of the Council was altered so as to give equal standing to academic, public and special libraries. The year 1962 saw the first working of the reorganized body and, after a few teething troubles, the new arrangements began to meet the needs of the expanding profession. The present list of groups and sections includes, as well as the Association of Assistant Librarians, those for Branch and Mobile Libraries, Cataloguing and Indexing, Colleges, Institutes and Schools of Education, Colleges of Technology and Further Education, County Libraries, Hospital Libraries and Handicapped Readers, Industrial Librarians, International and Comparative Librarianship, Library Education, Library History, Medical Libraries, Rare Books, Reference, Special and Information Section, Sound Recordings, University, College and Research, and Youth Libraries.

Every member is allowed to join two groups of the Association without extra payment. All the groups hold regular meetings, most of them hold an annual conference, they issue publications, they are organized nationally and regionally, and they have representation on the Council of the Library Association.

The Library Association is also organized regionally, with its twelve branches. These are, in alphabetical order, the Berkshire, Buckinghamshire and Oxfordshire, the East Midland, the Eastern, the London and Home Counties, the Northern, the North Western, the Northern Ireland, the South Western, the West Midland and the Yorkshire branches. Scotland is covered by the Scottish Library Association, and Wales by the Welsh Library Association, both of which have the status of branches. All the branches are governed by elected committees, they organize meetings and conferences, issue publications, and they too are represented on the LA Council. New members of the Association are automatically given branch membership without further payment or formality.

The Library Association Council is the governing body of the organization and it meets four times a year. The Committees of the Council are the Executive, Education, National, Academic and Medical, Publications, Public Libraries, Research and Development, and Special Libraries committees. From 1965 the headquarters of the Library Association has been at 7 Ridgmount Street, London WCIE 7AE.

In accordance with its Royal Charter, the Association maintains a good library, in which plans, illustrations, slides and tape-recordings do much to augment the many books and journals covering aspects of librarianship. The library is, of course, open to all members: books can be lent by post, and information is given by letter, telephone, or telex. The Catalogue of the LA Library was published in 1958 and is still a useful aid. Publications issued by the Association include the *Library Association Record* (monthly), *Library and Information Science Abstracts* (bi-monthly), the *Journal of Librarianship* (quarterly), the *Library and Information Bulletin* (irregular), *British Humanities Index* (quarterly with annual cumulations), *British Technology Index* (monthly with annual cumulations), the *Students' Handbook* (annually), and the *Library Association Year Book* (annually).

The Association's Publications Committee is very active and forward-looking and in addition to these regular publications, it issues special subject lists and bibliographies, the LA pamphlet series, the British text of the Anglo-American Cataloguing Rules, and such fine individual titles as Walford's *Guide to Reference Material*, Kelly's *Early Public Libraries*, Kaufman's *Libraries and their Users*, and the McColvin Festschrift, *Libraries for the People*, edited by R. F. Vollans.

The work of the Association's Education Committee also merits close attention. Successive committees have demonstrated an eager desire to keep at least abreast, and sometimes ahead of current developments, with the result that there have been frequent changes of syllabus in the past. The Education Committee, and the LA Council, have also done much to help to found and to further the progress of the fifteen library schools in the United Kingdom. Until the late 1960s, apart from University College, London, the Library Association was the sole examining body, but in recent years an increasing number of library schools carry out their own examining of students, though admission to the professional register of chartered librarians is still the prerogative of the Library Association.

From 1964 the current syllabus of general professional examinations came into operation. This consists of two examinations, named Part I and Part II respectively. The former consists of four three-hour papers, to be taken at one and the same sitting. These are:

1. The Library and the community.
2. Government and control of libraries.
3. The organization of knowledge.
4. Bibliographical control and service.

The minimum requirement for passing the Part II (Final) Examination is six papers of three hours each, which may be taken together or separately, and in any order. In this examination there are three lists, lettered A, B and C. Only one paper may be selected from List A, and one or more papers from Lists B and C. The full lists may be consulted in the LA *Students' Handbook*.

There is also a Post-Graduate Professional Examination consisting of five compulsory papers and two optional papers. Two of the compulsory papers consist of internally examined and externally assessed course-work, and certain optional papers also require course-work. The Post-Graduate Professional Examination will be passed or failed as a whole, though the Board of Assessors may allow candidates to be referred in papers at their discretion.

After passing the Part II Examination or the Post-Graduate Professional Examination, the student will be admitted to the Register of Chartered Librarians as an Associate of the Library Association, provided that he has completed three years' approved library service and has been a member of the Library Association for at least two years. At least one of the years of approved library service must come after meeting the examination requirements. Up to a maximum of one year spent on a full-time librarianship course is accepted as approved service, as also is any period of attachment to a single library whilst on a course, providing that it is not less than eight weeks in duration.

In recent years the Library Association has made provision for the admission to the Charter of mature practitioners, and for details of the requirements readers should refer to the *Library Association Year Book* or better still, to the Library Association itself.

Before leaving the Library Association special mention must be made of the work of some of its groups and branches. The AAL used to organize correspondence courses for the LA examinations and it still publishes a useful series of primers and other works of value to students of library science. The County Libraries Group issues a series of readers' guides on a variety of subjects: these are authoritative, attractive and cheap. The Reference, Special and Information Section issues guides to library resources in various parts of the country, while many Groups and Sections publish regular journals such as *SLA News* (from the Scottish Library Association), *Catalogue and Index* (from the Cataloguing and Indexing Group), *Book Trolley* (from the Hospital Libraries and Handicapped Readers Group), *Library History* (from the Library History Group), and *YLG News* (from the Youth Libraries Group).

In addition, the Branches and Groups regularly publish the proceedings and reports of conferences which they organize either on a regular basis or from time to time.

ASLIB

The organization we know as Aslib was founded in 1924 under the name of the Association of Special Libraries and Information Bureaux, but this title was abandoned in 1949, since when Aslib has been its official designation. The need for such a body arose because of the growth of specialist libraries and research organizations after the First World War, plus the fact that the Library Association was in those days slow to recognize the special needs of these bodies. Although much criticism has been directed against those who governed the Library Association at that time, it is more than likely that an organization such as Aslib would inevitably have been set up sooner or later, whatever action the LA had taken. In this connection it is noteworthy that the Americans found it necessary to establish a Special Libraries Association in their country.

The growth of Aslib has proved conclusively the need for such an organization. It now has over 2,500 members whereas before the Second World War it had only about 300, and its wide appeal is demonstrated by the fact that it includes in its membership national and public libraries, industrial and commercial firms, learned societies, universities, colleges, Government departments and individuals concerned with research and information services.

It was during the Second World War that Aslib really became recognized as an essential body, and that the foundations were laid for its expansion. The varied work it accomplished for the Government during the war led to its being given an annual grant through the Department of Scientific and Industrial Research. These continued grants, coupled with the increased membership, led to a great expansion of the work undertaken regularly by Aslib. In addition to its valuable publications, which will be described in the next paragraph, Aslib has a comprehensive library with information and consultant services. This library of special librarianship, information science and documentation techniques now contains upwards of 25,000 volumes and has files of 350 journals.

Aslib also maintains a translations index, so that duplication of effort may be avoided, and panels of translators and indexers are kept. Another activity is the documentary reproduction service, whereby Aslib will provide photocopies or microfilms of original documents in libraries. Aslib has branches in Scotland, the North of England and the Midlands, as well as eleven groups on such subjects as aeronautics, food and agriculture, textiles and so on. Both the national organization and the branches arrange regular meetings, while an annual residential conference is a feature of the Aslib calendar.

The first major publication of the association was the *Aslib Directory: A Guide to Sources of Specialist Information*, which was issued in 1928 with the help of a grant from the CUKT, and a second edition in two volumes came out in 1957. The current edition, the third, is also in two volumes, edited by Brian J. Wilson. Volume 1, covering information sources in science, technology and commerce, was published in 1968 and Volume 2, covering information sources in medicine, the social sciences and the humanities, came out in 1970.

Aslib's regular publications include the *Journal of Documentation*, devoted to the techniques of recording, organizing and disseminating information, and *Aslib Proceedings*, containing papers and reports of Aslib meetings and conferences. The *Aslib Booklist* is also a periodical publication, being a useful list of recently published scientific and technical books. Other publications include the *Aslib Membership List* and the *Index to Theses*, a classified list of the titles of theses accepted for higher degrees in British and Irish universities. From time to time Aslib also issues other books, and particular mention should be made of the *Handbook of Special Librarianship and Information Work*, edited by W. Ashworth, now in its third edition.

Aslib played a leading part in the projects of the *British Union Catalogue of Periodicals* (see p. 151) and the *British National Bibliography*. In 1959 the association took the lease of a new headquarters at 3 Belgrave Square, London, SW1X 8PL.

SCONUL

In 1950 a separate body was formed in the United Kingdom devoted to the special interests and problems of national and university libraries. This was called the Standing Conference on National and University Libraries, SCONUL for short. From the outset membership was by invitation, and although each member library is represented by its principal librarian, the British Museum Library has in fact four representatives, while the Bodleian Library and the Cambridge University Library each have two.

Other libraries in membership include the National Libraries of Scotland, Wales and Ireland, the NCL, the NLL, the John Rylands Library, and many other national, university and college libraries. Normally two meetings are held each year, and a number of sub-committees have been formed, among them those concerned with the Export of Printed Books and

Manuscripts, Co-operation in Acquisitions, Training for Librarianship, and Documentation. Despite the fact that the main body meets only twice a year, SCONUL has been extremely active through its sub-committees. It has organized courses of training for members of national and university library staffs, has given support to various projects relating to the locations and microfilming of manuscripts, and has sponsored the publication of David Ramage's *Finding-List of English Books to 1640*. Statistics, library co-operation, copyright, buildings and many other topics have featured in the conference programme, and SCONUL's achievements to date have fully justified its existence.

SCHOOL LIBRARY ASSOCIATION

The School Library Association was set up in 1937 to promote the development of libraries in schools, to ensure efficient administration, to provide opportunities for school librarians to meet and discuss mutual problems, and to make contact with other bodies having similar interests. Like the LA and Aslib it has formed branches in various parts of the country, meetings are held regularly, and a library for members has been formed. Its headquarters is located at 150 Southampton Row, London, WCIB 5 AR, and it issues free to members a publication called *The School Librarian,* which is published every school term.

OTHER BRITISH LIBRARY ORGANIZATIONS

It should not be thought that the associations described above are the sum total of organized activity in British librarianship. There are numerous other organizations which students should know about, although at an early stage in their studies it is perhaps not necessary to describe them in detail. Among these are the Circle of State Librarians, the Society of Indexers, the Society of County Librarians, the Microfilm Association of Great Britain, the Institute of Information Scientists, and the Association of British Library Schools. There is also the Society of Municipal and County Chief Librarians, though this is a registered trade union, and is concerned with salaries and service conditions rather than with professional affairs.

FOREIGN LIBRARY ASSOCIATIONS

Again it may not be essential for the newcomer to the profession to know details about library associations outside the United Kingdom, but it should be at least appreciated that most countries now have national associations devoted to the organization of library and information studies in their own areas. Outstanding among these is the American Library Association, founded in 1876, with its headquarters in Chicago. Other notable examples are the Canadian Library Association, the Library Association of Australia, the South African Library Association, the New Zealand Library Association, and the Library Association of Ireland. Library associations are also thriving in Denmark, Finland, Norway, Sweden, Romania, Belgium, the Netherlands, France, and East and West Germany. Even the smallest nations have found it necessary to establish such bodies, and librarians everywhere watch with interest the growth of such bodies as the Icelandic Librarians' Association, the Iranian Library Association and the Malta Library Association. Those interested in comparative librarianship will find a useful list of overseas library associations, not necessarily complete, in the current edition of the *Library Association Year Book.*

One of the newest international bodies to be formed is the Commonwealth Library Association (COMLA) which was started in November 1972. Its members are drawn from twenty-one countries of the Commonwealth and it will study common problems relating to staff education, book supply and other matters.

Chaper 6
Personnel management in libraries

As we have seen, libraries are usually governed by boards or committees, which are responsible for policy and management. The persons responsible for translating that policy into action are the librarian and the members of his staff. It is hardly an exaggeration to say that the success or otherwise of a library depends almost entirely on the quality and expertise of its staff. The best-stocked library in the world cannot give a comprehensive service to its users if it does not at the same time possess a keen, efficient and trained staff to exploit the stock to its fullest advantage.

The constant aim of the staff, whether in lending, children's, reference or information work should be to put the right book or the right information into the hands of the user. A great deal of tact is necessary in staff–public relations: librarians should be careful not to go too far in recommending books to readers, but on the other hand they should ensure that no person requiring help in the choice of books and other materials, or in procuring information from the library's contents, should go without that assistance. The good librarian or assistant librarian should therefore be something of a psychologist, able quickly to assess readers' individual personalities and requirements, and possessing the necessary tact and bibliographical knowledge to deal with each user according to his individual needs.

Equally desirable is a sound general education with a flair for keeping up-to-date with world events for, rightly or wrongly, readers expect librarians to have an almost cosmological knowledge. Like the good journalist, the good librarian should know something about everything, and everything about some things.

Knowledge of library stock and the question of assistance to readers is a subject complete in itself, and one which the student librarian will meet in his examinations. It is mentioned here in passing, because this problem of assistance, and how far library staff should go in rendering it, is one that should be considered by every student librarian at an early stage in his training.

STAFF ORGANIZATION AND DUTIES

Library staffs range in size from three or four in the smallest special libraries to those of hundreds in the largest national and public libraries. This factor of size, as well as the fact that conditions vary from library to library, make it impossible to lay down too precisely the duties of the various grades of staff. For example, the duties of a chief librarian in a large local authority will differ in some ways from those of a college librarian or the head of a Government department library. But some common ground can be traced, and the attempt will be made to outline some of the accepted duties of the different grades of library personnel.

The *chief librarian* or *director*, as he is sometimes now known, will in general be fully occupied with decisions on internal professional policy, committee work, and administration in the most general sense. He will be concerned from time to time with matters of establishment – promotions, new appointments, additions and deletions to the staff, study facilities, leave of absence. All these and other personnel matters will be his concern as he prepares his recommendations to the committee or governing body of the library. He has to view the service as a whole, and he may find it necessary to recommend the provision of a new building or buildings. If these are agreed he will have to work in close collaboration with architects.

At all times he will have to work closely with the legal and financial departments of his concern, whether it be a city, a county, a Government department, a university, a school, a hospital or an industrial organization. He must be accessible both to members of his governing body and to users of his library, and he must conduct his correspondence with speed and courtesy. He must be adept at writing reports, being brief and to the point, yet capable of giving prominence to the salient points and, if necessary, of offering a confident recommendation. As well as taking a global view of the service he should, like a

6

good general, have an eye for detail and keep a constant eye on matters of routine, so that his staff do not become bogged down with unnecessary work. In these days of organization and method, the chief librarian will almost certainly come into contact with experts on management services. If his governing body has decided to employ such experts, it is the duty of the chief librarian to co-operate fully with them and to give them the fullest possible information. He often has a chance to discuss their report before it is finalized, and good management consultants will usually give full consideration to the chief librarian's views, even though they may not always accept them in full.

In short, the work of the chief librarian is essential to the success of the library he serves. It is his job to obtain, through his reports and discussions, the necessary budgets to ensure the efficient running of the service. He should also be a good 'front man', a real link between his governing body, his users and his staff. He is, in every sense of the word, a director, and it is perhaps no accident that this nomenclature is being increasingly applied to him.

The post of *deputy librarian* normally exists in all but the smallest libraries, and there is a fair measure of agreement as to what his duties should entail. Briefly, these are to take the place of the chief librarian in his absence, to organize the general routine of the library, to supervise the staff and to deal with establishment matters such as interviews, appointments, resignations, time-sheets and leave of absence. He is often also responsible for preparing the details of capital and revenue budgets, and has to liaise frequently with his opposite numbers in the legal, financial, engineering and architectural divisions of his concern. There should be the closest possible collaboration with his chief, since deputizing for him means that the deputy librarian must be *au fait* with everything that is happening in the library complex, and should also be familiar with his chief's intentions regarding future developments. Not only should he confer with his chief regularly, he should also attend all committee meetings and see all correspondence entering and leaving the department. The deputy librarian should also keep a watchful eye on the staff generally, for he often has to act as a bridge between the staff and the chief librarian.

Larger library systems, whether they be national, academic or public libraries, find it necessary to have various divisions in their staff hierarchies, each with a head or librarian-in-charge. In a medium-sized public library system, for example, these may be confined to lending, reference and children's divisions, but in systems of larger compass there will probably be separate departments for music, commerce, technology, foreign languages, local history and archives, and the librarians-in-charge of these will figure as departmental or divisional heads, each being fully responsible to the chief librarian for the successful running and development of the particular aspect of the service. In these bigger systems it is also often found essential to have separate divisions for bibliographical services and for general administration. The main concerns of these departmental heads are the organization of routines, staff duties, and the selection of books and other materials for their particular divisions.

Each library will have its own staff hierarchy according to its needs. It must be remembered, however, that many of the larger libraries, academic or public, are subject-departmental-ized, in which case there may be a somewhat different staff organization to that mentioned above. In the subject-departmentalized library, each department must be in the charge of a qualified librarian who is also a subject specialist. Often, though not always, these subject specialists will be equal in rank under the chief and the deputy librarian.

In public libraries the post of *district* or *branch librarian* is extremely important, since the holder is the representative of the chief librarian, and indeed of the library authority in the area served by his library. It is largely upon his ability and personality that the standing of the library service in that district depends and is judged by the community. The librarian-in-charge of a district or branch library will be responsible for the control of his own staff but, owing to the centralization of acquisitions, classifying and cataloguing which now obtains in most systems, he will have little real scope except in the matter of personal service to readers and in such extension work as exhibitions, lectures, concerts and other activities. Although book ordering will almost certainly be organized centrally, it is customary for the district or branch librarian to participate in book selection. He is the one person who knows the reading needs of his library's users and his expertise should be fully drawn upon.

All the library's technical processes such as ordering, accessioning, classifying, cataloguing and interlibrary loans will normally be centralized. This requires a separate division under its own head, and such a division is often called the bibliographical services or bibliographical control division. Since the advent of computer-produced catalogues this side of the library's work calls for a knowledge of what computers can and cannot do, and it also predicates a willingness to accept new ideas and to collaborate with experts in computers and other sophisticated machinery.

One other division of library work must be mentioned and that is the administration. In these days of larger library units it is all the more necessary that library administration should be exact and uniform throughout the system. Such a division will be in the charge of a senior administrative officer who will be aided by as many clerks and typists as are needed. This section will have to deal with salaries and wages, the ordering and recording of stationery and supplies, the multifarious duties in connection with the repair and maintenance of buildings, and many other administrative tasks. An efficient division of this kind can relieve the chief and the deputy librarian of a great deal of minutiae, leaving them more free to view the system as a whole and to plan its development.

Some miscellaneous elements of staff provision include posts of training officer, public relations officer and display artists. These are all vitally necessary in larger library systems. Where they appear in the staff hierarchy is a matter for local decision. Since the training officer and the public relations officer are pervasive to the system as a whole they sometimes operate directly under the chief librarian or his deputy. Public relations is a field in which libraries need to operate more energetically than they have in the past, and it is interesting to note that more and more libraries are employing people on PR work. Some have public relations librarians, that is, qualified librarians responsible for PR work and development, while others prefer to employ a person untrained in librarianship but experienced in the PR field.

The last but by no means least element in library staffs are the junior assistants, or clerks as they are known in American and some European libraries. The work allotted to personnel on this grade may sometimes be regarded as monotonous but it is certainly not valueless. On the contrary, they carry out some of the most important tasks in the library. The alleged monotony of a library assistant's life is only a half-truth, and much depends on his or her attitude to the job. If the assistant is really interested in books and in people the tasks will be found far from boring.

Senior librarians and those responsible for organizing routine work in the library can, however, make a notable contribution to staff harmony and interest if they ensure that the most monotonous routine tasks are fairly distributed, and that junior assistants are not kept too long on work of this kind. In the main, a library assistant's work consists of service desk duties, charging and discharging books, shelving returned books, keeping the shelves tidy and orderly, preparing readers' tickets and book cards, dealing with reservations, sending overdue notices and checking the receipt of periodicals. As a rule, the smaller the library the greater the variety of tasks which are allotted to assistants.

It should be impressed on junior personnel from the outset that they have a vital part to play in the public relations of the library. They are often the first people that a library user meets, and their courtesy, intelligence and general reception of patrons can work wonders for the good name of the service.

STAFF HANDBOOKS AND INSTRUCTIONS

The two chief virtues, and indeed essentials, in library administration and procedures are accuracy and uniformity. One of the best ways to ensure uniformity in the work of the library is to start a file of staff instructions. Such manuals will usually begin with the general, such as laying down the responsibility for the various departments and the duties of staff, and proceed to the particular, such as dealing with the precise ways in which books shall be prepared for circulation and use. Examples of some of the other subjects on which guidance can be given are:

custody of keys, fire precautions, action to be taken in case of fire, disturbances, illness to users, etc., readers' registration, sending of overdue notices, the reservation system, interlibrary loan routines, readers' requests, binding procedures, classification decisions, cataloguing styles, interavailability of readers' tickets and so on.

The file of staff instructions should be read and initialled by all members of the staff, although some libraries make a practice of issuing a copy of the staff manual to all personnel. The intention of the staff manual is simply to try to ensure uniformity of procedures. Such a file provides a most convenient way of acquainting new assistants with the methods employed. If it is kept in loose-leaf form it is a simple matter to add new instructions as and when they become necessary, or to replace out-dated instructions with new ones. Staff instructions have been a feature of many public, academic and special libraries, and it is noteworthy that such a library as the Bodleian has found it advantageous to maintain a staff manual in printed form for many years.

Rather different from the staff manual or instruction file is the staff handbook. A number of libraries now produce such a handbook, the intention of which is to provide a brief guide to new members of staff on such practical matters as service conditions, pay, holiday entitlements, training and education, including a general outline of the library service and what it is attempting to do. Such a handbook is a useful and time-saving device in large libraries where the staff turnover is considerable. The *Westminster City Libraries Staff Handbook* may be quoted as an example. After a welcoming foreword, it contains brief chapters on the City of Westminster, Staff, The Library Service, The Stock, Library Co-operation, and Library Publications. Appendices include such useful information as an outline of the classification system, branch code letters, locations of reserve stock, special subjects collected by the libraries, abbreviations in common use, and the staff organization chart.

As libraries and library systems grow in size, administrators ought to give favourable consideration to the preparation and circulation of staff handbooks of this kind.

PROFESSIONAL AND NON-PROFESSIONAL DUTIES

Most library administrators are agreed upon the desirability of the division of staffs into two distinct grades: professional and non-professional. The majority of the larger libraries apply this principle, but difficulties arise in applying the idea in smaller and medium-sized libraries. The trend towards the division is however inevitable and has been hastened by two developments, first the increasing number of larger systems and secondly, the increasing use of automation in which computers and other machinery is being employed.

Some time ago the Library Association studied this problem and issued a report in 1962 under the title of *Professional and Non-professional Duties in Libraries*. This listed, very thoroughly and clearly, duties in all types of libraries and classified them into professional and other grades. It has been used as a basis by many libraries, and it is shortly to be revised to bring it into line with recent developments in library science.

SALARIES AND CONDITIONS OF SERVICE

Time was when there was little uniformity in the salaries, hours and working conditions of the staffs of either public, academic or special libraries, and the Association of Assistant Librarians was one of the bodies which prepared reports in an effort to improve conditions generally. These attempts have been reasonably successful, and few library staff can now complain that their hours and conditions of service are in any way Dickensian. Salaries, either in Government, academic and public libraries, are now agreed nationally, and arbitration is called in when disputes occur. Salaries in special libraries still give cause for concern, but this is a difficult problem because special libraries come under many different headings. The Library Association, through its Special Libraries Committee, is giving attention to this problem and is collecting data in the hope that some basis may be found for recommended salary scales in special libraries.

Every librarian or assistant should know thoroughly the service conditions under which he works, and nationally agreed schemes such as that produced by the National Joint Council for Local Authorities' Administrative, Professional, Technical and Clerical Services. This particular scheme, first issued in 1946 and revised many times since, inaugurated the thirty-eight-hour week for all local government staffs, laid down salary scales for the various grades of personnel, and made conditions relating to sickness, holiday entitlements, subsistence and travelling expenses, study leave and other eventualities. In all public libraries, personnel are therefore working a thirty-eight-hour week, the only variations between library and library being the particular time-sheet worked.

Service to the public is always the prime consideration in the operation of a time-sheet, but it will make for a contented staff if a time-sheet can be devised which avoids split-duties and which affords a reasonable rota of free Saturdays. In many non-public libraries a five-day working week is possible so that all Saturdays are free, but in public libraries Saturdays are often the busiest days of the week. The compilation of a time-sheet is by no means an easy task, but it is important to bear in mind that adequate staffing of all departments must be maintained so that queues of users can be avoided. Due allowance must also be made for meal-times. As far as possible these should be kept the same for each person throughout the week. Finally, there should be close observance of the thirty-eight-hour week, or whatever the agreed hours are, so that overtime may be avoided.

STAFF TRAINING AND QUALIFICATION

Promotion in librarianship depends upon the assistant becoming a qualified librarian, through possession either of the Library Association qualification or one of the degrees or diplomas now directly awarded by library schools. Every ambitious student must aim for one or other of these qualifications.

Education in librarianship in the United Kingdom has changed rapidly and radically since the last edition of this book. There are now fifteen library schools in the country as a whole, these being located at Aberdeen, Aberystwyth, Belfast, Birmingham, Brighton, Glasgow, Leeds, Liverpool, Loughborough, Manchester, Newcastle, Sheffield, and three in London. Up-to-date details of their full names and addresses, and courses offered, can always be found in the current edition of the *Students' Handbook* published by the Library Association. Every aspirant should obtain a personal copy of this essential booklet, and should study it carefully. Comparison can be made of the different courses offered by the various library schools, so that the student can make his own choice. Early application to the school or schools of one's selection must be made, since there is now great competition for places. Applicants are interviewed to judge their suitability. The courses are comprehensive and are presented by well-qualified lecturers. The programmes include interesting visits to libraries of different types and sizes, to binderies and to other relevant establishments.

The previously mentioned *Students' Handbook* contains full details of the Library Association syllabus of examinations, around which the library school courses are built. At one time University College, London, was the only school offering an independent diploma and conducting its own examinations, but radical changes have taken place in education for librarianship in recent years. The Library Association now permits most of the library schools to conduct their own examinations, though the ultimate qualification of chartered librarian is still granted by the LA. Most of the library schools now offer both the one-year post-graduate course and the two-year non-graduate course, though it is important to note that some of the university schools offer only the post-graduate course. Degrees in library science are now a feature of some of the schools, ranging from the M.A. in Librarianship at the University of Sheffield to the B.A. in Librarianship (CNAA) at Newcastle upon Tyne and other library schools.

Correspondence courses, once a prominent feature of library education, have disappeared from the scene, and part-time courses, which were valuable before the library schools developed to their present standard, have dwindled almost entirely. But useful adjuncts to library education still exist in the form of the Scottish Summer School, held annually at Newbattle Abbey College, and the Youth Libraries Group's annual Weekend School. Details of these are to be found in the LA

Students' Handbook. Many occasional weekend schools and
conferences are also organized by the various Branches and
Groups of the Library Association, and aspirants should keep a
watchful eye on the pages of the *Library Association Record* for
announcements of these.

As library systems have grown in size, more of them have
found it possible to include a training officer or officers on their
staff establishments. In most good libraries, 'in-service' training,
as it is called, has been practised for many years. This calls for
precise and careful organization so, with the larger staffs
employed today, a training officer is essential.

While librarians-in-charge will obviously still be responsible
for job training, it is vitally necessary to carry out basic training
courses which will try to give the newcomer an outline view of
the work of the library system as a whole. The training officer
will himself give talks of a general nature, using the seminar
approach for the greater involvement of his audience. But the
consequent programme will bring in the heads of senior
librarians from the various sections, such as bibliographical
services, reference services or audio-visual services. It may also
be found necessary to organize refresher courses at a later date,
not only for junior members of the staff but for newly qualified
librarians as well. The number of courses organized, and their
duration, must of course be influenced by practical considerations such as the availability of staff to attend courses and the
availability, too, of the senior librarians who take part as
tutors.

The duties of the training officer may also include interviewing and appointing junior personnel, and arranging
programmes for visiting student librarians who are on fieldwork from library schools. It is also appropriate for the training
officer to be in charge of the professional library of library
science materials. For despite the fact that the schools have
good professional collections, it is perhaps more than ever
necessary that libraries should provide their own staffs with
up-to-date collections on library science, including books,
journals, pamphlets, illustrations and other materials.

STAFF INTERCHANGES

Experience in different types and sizes of libraries is of great value, and experiments which have taken place with the interchange of staff between libraries have usually proved very successful and of lasting value. Efforts to set up organized schemes of staff interchange between libraries in the United Kingdom have, however, usually broken down owing to legal and financial complications, to say nothing of the difficulties of finding suitable living accommodation for staff working far from their own homes.

Individual interchanges are generally encouraged by public librarians and local authorities, but it should be borne in mind that as public libraries are increasingly standardized in the United Kingdom today, the fullest benefit from an interchange may perhaps be obtained when the participants are from different types of libraries, i.e. from public to special, or from academic to public libraries. The absence of an official scheme of interchange should not deter the keen aspirant if he really wishes to have practical experience in another library. He should approach his training officer or chief librarian, and arrangements may be made on an individual basis for the idea to be translated into practice.

Staff interchange on an international level might be thought to be even more difficult, though in fact many such exchanges have taken place. In recent years the Library Association initiated a scheme of internships whereby young librarians from overseas are enabled to work for one year in British libraries. Library associations in the United States have also received British librarians in the same way. International staff exchanges have also been arranged under the auspices of INTAMEL. At the time of writing, financial stringency has cut down the possibility of internships, though a few opportunities are still available. International exchanges of staff have, however, been of such outstanding value that we must hope for an early resumption on an even larger scale.

STAFF MEETINGS AND STAFF ASSOCIATIONS

Most chief librarians find it necessary to hold periodical staff meetings of senior librarians to acquaint them with developments and projects, and to discuss ideas they may have for the betterment of the service. In larger libraries such a practice is essential and has been a feature for many years. Staff meetings of this kind should be properly constituted with regular agenda and minutes circulated by a senior librarian appointed as secretary.

Staff associations are a feature of many large and medium-sized systems. Membership should be open to all those on the staff, but these organizations are not trade unions. They should be more concerned with social, welfare and off-duty activities. Sometimes they issue a staff bulletin or magazine which is circulated to all members. Staff associations are to be encouraged, for their activities can be very helpful in welding a staff together, especially when the system comprises many branches and departments. Their programmes often include dinners, theatre visits, vocational visits, day outings and the like.

APPOINTMENTS, APPLICATIONS AND INTERVIEWS

Appointments in libraries in the United Kingdom are usually publicly advertised, the appropriate periodical to search being *The Times Literary Supplement*. Advertisements for positions in public, academic and special libraries may also be found in the *Library Association Record*, *The Times*, the *Guardian* and the *Daily Telegraph*.

Applying for publicly advertised posts is an art that should be carefully studied. Often the advertisement asks the applicant to send for an application form: this cramps the style of the applicant somewhat, but at least it ensures that he provides the information wanted, and there is usually an opportunity to add further details if necessary. When application forms are not provided, the candidate should, if possible, type his application.

Long paragraphs of prose are not required in an application: instead, it should be tabulated in numbered paragraphs with such headings as name, address, age, date of birth, education, present post, previous posts, and general experience. Copies of testimonials are sometimes called for, but it is more usual for applicants to be asked to give the names and addresses of two referees. These referees will only be approached if the applicant is to be interviewed for the post. But if copies of testimonials are required, see that these too are neatly typed. The importance of neat and striking presentation cannot be over-emphasized.

If the post is a desirable one there will probably be many applicants, and a short-list will be selected for interview on a certain date and at a certain time. It has been truly said that the object of the application is to secure an interview, and the objective at the interview is to secure the appointment. The interviewing board may consist of about three senior librarians. Beforehand, the candidate will presumably have learnt as much as he can about the library where he hopes to work. Reference books will supply some of this information, and more may be gleaned by a visit to the library before the interview.

Although it is difficult to avoid being nervous at an interview, the best candidates are those who can at least give the appearance of nervelessness. Try to anticipate as many questions as possible, and rehearse the answers. On the other hand, be ready for the type of interview which is more common these days – the type where the candidate is asked to address the interviewing board on his experience and why he is seeking the post. This calls for self-salesmanship of a high order and the applicant's modesty has to be forgotten for the duration of the interview. At any interview, appear neatly dressed, and be ready to answer precisely such questions as your present salary and when you could start work with your new authority. If appointed, do not forget to thank the interviewing board for their confidence in you.

Chapter 7
Library departments and methods

This chapter deals with departmental routine in libraries, and though the emphasis is on public libraries, many of the methods described are also applicable in libraries of other types. It must be clearly understood that in such a small compass each aspect can only be dealt with in outline, and it is more than ever necessary for the student librarian to undertake additional reading, details of which will be found at the end of this book. In addition to information on methodology in circulation, reference and children's libraries, some description is given of the routines used in mobile libraries, audio-visual work, and periodicals areas.

CIRCULATION WORK

By circulation work we mean the methods called for in the lending of books and other materials. It involves the registration of readers, methods of loan, procedures for renewals and overdue books, methods of dealing with readers' requests and reservations, and other services.

Libraries which lend books find it necessary to ask readers to complete a simple form of application, recent trends having all been directed towards cutting formalities and requirements to a minimum. Some allow all persons to become users on their own signatures, but others still require a countersignature in the form of a guarantee, especially when the reader is a child, a student or a non-resident employee.

In each case, when the completed application form is received, it is checked and verified, the reader's ticket or tickets are made out and issued, and the application form is filed in alphabetical order. Libraries used to make readers wait for a day or two until these formalities had been completed, and some regrettably still do this, but most now permit users to begin borrowing material immediately. To make readers wait, or to ask them to pay another visit to the library on another day before they can borrow books and audio-visual material, is merely to place an irritating obstacle in their paths, and is a continuation of that petty officialdom which the best of modern librarians have striven to abolish in their libraries.

When gramophone records and other audio-visual materials began to be a feature of public libraries, it was customary to regard this as a separate entity, and users were often asked to complete a separate application form before borrowing this type of material. Now, however, many libraries use a single application form, simply asking the reader if he wishes to borrow these materials as well as books.

While everyone wishes to reduce formalities to a minimum, the librarian still has a duty to his authority to protect the library and other readers from the results of misuse and mal-practices. This is why verification of the details submitted on the application form is still necessary, and it is also essential to maintain a defaulters' file. This is an alphabetical index of the names and addresses of readers who have failed to return borrowed material. The authors, titles and prices of the non-returned books are also listed on the cards, and all new applications are normally checked with this file, to try to avoid re-admitting readers who have not settled their debts with the library.

People who are employed or who attend educational establishments in the area of the library authority are by law allowed to use all the facilities of the library, even if they reside outside the area. People who neither live, work or study in the library's area are allowed to register for borrowing on payment of an annual subscription, the amount of which is fixed by the library authority. In many areas this does not arise, since many neighbouring authorities have accepted the principle of interavailability, whereby a resident of one area may use the library services of a neighbouring area, and vice versa. The London boroughs, for example, have a complete interavailability scheme. Yet another way of allowing outside readers to use a library is to have a financial agreement between neighbouring library authorities, so that a fixed sum is paid to the host authority for each outside reader registered. Finally, most holiday resorts accept current library tickets from any- where in the United Kingdom, and indeed the situation is rapidly arising that most libraries will accept tickets from, and issue material to visitors to their areas, even though they have no obligation to do so under the Public Libraries and Museums Act of 1964.

Another detail of some importance in connection with the registration of readers is to ensure that addresses are kept up-to- date. Readers should be reminded of the need to inform the library of changes of address, and these should be recorded both on the readers' tickets and on the original application forms. To assist in keeping the records of users' addresses reasonably up-to-date renewals of registration are sometimes required. The period of availability is a matter for the individual library, but it should not be too frequent since busy people are justifiably annoyed if they are asked too often to repeat the formality of re-registering.

Practice varies on the question of how many books, gramo- phone records or other material may be taken out by users at any one time. Some charging systems have in any event little or no control over this, but libraries on the Browne or token charging systems can control this, and a decision has to be made on how many tickets or tokens are issued to each user. One influencing factor is whether the stock of the library is large enough to permit the issue of unlimited material to users. Some control was perhaps necessary when library stocks were less adequate than they now are, but now that stocks are generally better material can be issued more generously. Students especially should be given generous treatment; extra tickets and extended loan periods should be granted to those who request them for specific purposes. The only stipulation to extended loan periods is that material should be returned on demand if it has been reserved by other users. Public libraries, far from putting obstacles in the way of users, should go out of their way to meet genuine and reasonable needs for books and other articles.

CHARGING SYSTEMS

The method of issuing books and other materials is known as a charging system. Since the advent of public libraries in the mid-nineteenth century there has been a variety of charging systems, including the Cotgreave indicator, the ledger method, the Newark system, the Detroit, Browne and Dickman systems, token charging, self-service methods, photocharging, punched card methods, Bookamatic and cheque-book charging, and there have also been combinations of some of the above. The evolution continues, since computerized charging has been introduced into some libraries in recent years.

Of those historic methods, the ledger and the indicator, nothing will be said, as information on them may be obtained, if required, from earlier textbooks. The Detroit, Newark and Dickman systems are American, and full descriptions can be found in Helen Geer's *Charging Systems*. The traditional method still in use in some British libraries is the Browne system. This involves equipping each book with a card which, when the book is issued, is placed inside the reader's ticket, the latter being in the form of a pocket. The charge, that is the reader's ticket with the book card inside it, is filed in trays according to the date of issue or return. The filing order is usually according to the book's accession number, though there are alternatives.

The Browne system is a speedy way of charging books, so little delay is experienced by users when they are taking material out of the library. The discharging procedure which takes place when they are returning material is, however, much slower, as tickets have to be sought from the many filing trays. As the use of public libraries grew rapidly in the mid-twentieth century, congestion was reported by many, and at no point in the library was congestion more noticeable than at the service desk, which was invariably too small.

No wonder that in the last twenty years librarians everywhere have been increasingly concerned with speedier techniques for charging books and other articles. Some libraries experimented with the delayed discharge of books, a temporizing method under which users were admitted into the library quickly at busy periods, leaving the actual discharging to be effected at later and slacker times. The cheque-book charging system was a variant of the idea of delayed discharge, but it is now not very common.

In the centre of large metropolitan cities a special problem was posed because a large number of office workers exchanged their books during the luncheon periods and the queues of readers waiting to hand in their books charged by the Browne method was intolerable. Nowhere was this more noticeable than at Westminster in the heart of London. To solve the problem, a token charging system was evolved. In addition to their readers' tickets, which have to be produced at every transaction, users were given a number of tokens. A token is surrendered whenever a book is borrowed, and a token is given back to the user whenever he returns a book. Since it effectively abolished queues the system was considered successful, though it has some drawbacks, the chief one being that the whereabouts of the stock is not known under the system. The idea has worked well at Westminster, but the scheme was not recommended for export. Despite this warning, some other libraries adopted the token system, often with variations. One common variation was to limit the use of tokens to fiction, leaving non-fiction to be issued by another method. Westminster itself will abandon the token system eventually in favour of a computerized method of charging.

Meanwhile, other librarians began to introduce photo-charging, which is still in use in many libraries in the United States, the United Kingdom, Scandinavia, Germany and else-where. With this system the usual date labels are dispensed with, and instead serially numbered transaction cards are used. Users are issued with a plastic ticket bearing name, address and date of expiry. At the exit desk, the reader's ticket, the book card (if used) and a transaction card are photographed on to 16 mm panchromatic film: the book card and transaction card are replaced in the book, while the reader retains his ticket. As well as being numbered, the transaction cards are serially lettered in order to facilitate tracing of books overdue. When the book is returned, a glance at the serial letter reveals whether or not an overdue charge has to be made. The reader passes into the library, and the transaction card is merely taken out of the book for refiling by letter and number. Overdues are dis-covered by checking the files of transaction cards, a process aided by machine sorting, while reserved books are checked with a visible index.

Reference has already been made to Helen Geer's *Charging Systems*, and another publication of interest to those who wish to study the comparative advantages and disadvantages of the various methods of charging is published by the Library Association. Edited by F. N. Hogg and others, this is entitled *Report on a Survey Made of Book Charging Systems at Present in Use in England*. Although issued in 1961 it is still of value because some of the systems are still in use. The only real development since that time has been the gradual introduction by some libraries of various computerized methods of charging.

Libraries are utilizing computers in numerous ways, and many librarians who have for years been searching for the ideal method of charging claim to have found this with the aid of the computer. Not only public libraries, but university and college libraries as well, have introduced forms of computerized charging. Indeed the universities, some of them, have led the way in experiment, helped by their own computer centres. In the United States, many academic and public libraries are operating computerized charging, while in the United Kingdom differing methods may be inspected at Chichester, Brighton, Camden and elsewhere.

RENEWALS AND OVERDUES

In most libraries the period of loan is now three weeks, though there are some variants, some being two weeks and others four weeks. Readers are nearly always allowed to renew books for further periods, if they are not reserved by other users. Renewals may be made by personal visit, by post or by telephone. Some libraries have installed telephone-answering services so that requests for renewals may be made at any time, being recorded and dealt with after playback.

To encourage the more frequent circulation of material, fines are usually charged on overdue books and other articles. In England and Wales this is specifically authorized by the Public Libraries and Museums Act of 1964, though it is not mandatory on library authorities. A few libraries do not levy any charges for overdue material, but the majority do in respect of adult readers, though not to children.

Libraries usually send regular reminders to users about overdue material. At one time it was common for three reminders to be sent, but the high cost of administration and postage, coupled with the increasing number of overdues, has resulted in libraries now sending only two reminders. If the user ignores these written appeals, which are usually in the form of folded circulars, a telephone call may be made, or sometimes a personal call at the reader's home. Finally, the recalcitrants are reported to the legal authority which usually sends letters threatening court action.

In order to attract the return of overdue books, some libraries have experimented with amnesty weeks, making it known that during a particular week no charges will be made on overdue material. The results have been mixed but, generally speaking, such weeks cannot be said to have been a great success, though they have had some general publicity value.

RESERVATIONS

It is common practice in public libraries to have a scheme whereby users may for a small fee reserve any book or other article which is not readily available at the time of asking. The fee is charged to cover the cost of notifying the user when the book is available for him. Some libraries do not accept reservations for fiction, but this restriction should be avoided if possible. When a user wishes to reserve a book or other article, his name and address is written on the front of a printed postcard, and on the reverse is written the details of the article required. All reservation cards are serially numbered and, in the case of books, filed in author order.

When books are returned they are checked to see if they have been reserved by other readers before they are returned to the shelves. If they are reserved, they are kept at the service desk, the reserve cards being extracted from the file and sent to the readers concerned. Books are usually kept for three or four days: if not then claimed they are either put back into circulation or, if still reserved, the next card on the list is sent. Both the photocharging and the token systems require the use of visible strip indexes for checking reserves. For this, it is best to have a sorting room adjacent to the service desk. Computerized charging systems have the great advantage of aiding reservation systems mechanically: they can also print out overdue notices.

OTHER SERVICES TO USERS

In the past few years many efforts have been made to give a really personal service to readers. The reservation system comes under this heading, as does the readers' request service. These are established ideas, but in recent times we have seen the advent of readers' advisers in libraries, qualified librarians specially detailed to deal with readers' book needs and queries. In addition, many libraries now provide a good deal of printed guidance.

New readers, for example, should be presented with a pamphlet detailing library facilities and privileges. Folders listing recent additions on a particular subject, or bulletins listing new books and other material are regularly published by some libraries. Nearly everywhere readers are encouraged to recommend books, while some libraries maintain indexes of readers' interests, enabling news of recent books on certain subjects to be sent to the readers who are known to be interested in those topics. Reading lists should be willingly compiled by librarians either for individual readers or for adult classes and societies and, as has already been suggested, extra borrowing facilities and extended periods of loan should be granted where possible to serious library users.

BRANCH AND MOBILE LIBRARIES

Nearly all public library services find it necessary to provide branch and mobile libraries in order to serve all the people living in their areas. While the routines at such service points must obviously conform to those at the main library, branch and mobile libraries call for distinct techniques, so much so that the Library Association now has a thriving Branch and Mobile Libraries Group, the members of which arrange meetings and issue publications dealing with common problems.

Mobile libraries, or bookmobiles as they are often called, are of special interest to students. They are either rigid vehicles or trailer-type vehicles, and they carry anything from 1,000 to 3,000 volumes depending on their size. The shelves face inwards and are tilted and rimmed to prevent books from falling off while the vehicle is in motion. A small service desk is fitted at one end of the vehicle and portable steps are carried, these being fitted into position when the bookmobile arrives at one of its scheduled stops.

County mobile libraries which serve areas with a scattered population may visit certain areas at long intervals, and when this is the case readers are allowed to take quite a number of books at each visit. In urban areas, bookmobiles work to a scheduled programme, visiting sites at fixed hours each week. These sites are usually marked with notices informing the public of the times and durations of the visits, and it is customary for a mains supply of electricity to provide the vehicles with lighting and heating during their sometimes long halts. Natural lighting is provided from toplights and these are usually hinged to provide ventilation in warm weather.

Bookmobiles need a centre from which to operate, and in which to accommodate the pool of stock from which their contents are replenished. They need, too, a separate librarian with as many additional librarians and assistants as are necessary to run the service efficiently. Books are issued in the same way as at the main and branch libraries, reservations and requests are received, overdues are sent from the operating centre, and generally the bookmobiles are just like additional branches. Bad weather can sometimes dislocate services and when this happens care must be taken to adjust charges for overdue books and to keep reserved books for a longer period so that readers do not suffer unduly.

No bookmobile can ever be as satisfactory as a permanent branch, but it is often the answer to the difficult problem of serving a number of perimeter areas none of which may be large enough to warrant a permanent library building. Bookmobiles have often been found useful in supplying rapidly growing areas, until such time as those areas can be supplied from a new permanent branch.

Mobile libraries are world-wide phenomena. Used for many years by American county libraries, they have also been a feature of library service in Denmark, Finland, Norway, Sweden and other European countries. Since the spread of public libraries in developing countries, their aid has been enlisted in virtually every part of the world. They have helped to spread the public library image in Africa, India, South America and many other places.

Nor are travelling libraries confined to the automobile. In Swedish Lapland a railbus is utilized, stopping at every isolated community along the line with its literary load. There are also bookboats, used by Bergen in Norway, Gothenburg and Stockholm in Sweden, and elsewhere. Where an archipelago with small settlements has to be served, the bookboat is the obvious answer.

AUDIO-VISUAL DEPARTMENTS

Audio-visual departments include learning material in such forms as gramophone records, cassettes, films, filmstrips, slides, photographs, prints, pictures and other media. They are more common in the United States than in Europe, but more examples of them are now occurring in European libraries with the growth of learning resources centres. The outstanding difference between American and European provision is that many libraries in the United States have large stocks of films for borrowing, while in Europe this is not generally the case. This has enabled American libraries to group audio materials with visual media into one convenient department.

In Britain and in many other European countries the emphasis since 1946 has been on the provision of gramophone record collections, either for loan as in the United Kingdom or for use in the library, as has been the main tendency in Scandinavian libraries. Recently, however, the Scandinavian librarians have developed an inclination to follow British and American practice by opening up their gramophone record libraries for home loans.

The first gramophone record collections consisted entirely of standard 78 r.p.m. discs, but about 1950 the first 33 r.p.m.

long-playing records began to appear, and librarians were
quick to start adding them to their collections. For a long time
all LP discs were monaural, but stereo was the next development
and once again librarians had to tackle the problem of gradually
replacing their monaural discs with the stereo type. LP records
are unbreakable, but they can be very easily damaged by
rough treatment or if they are played on a machine with a worn
or damaged stylus. The discs must be kept scrupulously clean,
and should be wiped with a barely damp cloth or sponge before
and after playing.

This susceptibility to damage means that a public gramophone record collection must have strict rules, and a ceaseless
propaganda is necessary in order that users do not ruin the
discs through careless, negligent or ignorant handling. It is
essential for gramophone record collections to be in the charge
of a qualified librarian, and all the staff who work there should
not only have a good knowledge of music and records, but
should also be tactful in their handling of the public. In this
department above all others it is essential that relations
between staff and public should be maintained at a high level.

The original gramophone record libraries used to operate on
closed access with the discs kept behind the staff service desk,
an indicator being used to show users which of the discs were
available for loan at the time of their visit. Some still operate
this way, owing to lack of space, but more now have an open
access system, allowing users to select their discs from browser
boxes. Experience has shown that discs are not damaged in
this way, and borrowers appreciate the opportunity to read
the information printed on the colourful and attractive
sleeves.

Before issue it is necessary for both the staff and users to
examine the discs and ensure that any existing damage is
agreed and marked. On return the discs are again examined by
the library staff. Records are catalogued with entries under
composers, titles and artistes, but the arrangement on the
presses or in the browser boxes is often, though not always, by
makers' numbers. Records are usually issued for the same
period as books in the library, and are renewable if not reserved. Reservations can be made in the usual way, and charges
are made for overdue discs.

One essential in the gramophone record library is a good reference section, consisting of files of *The Gramophone* and other relevant periodicals, makers' catalogues, and all the recognized reference books on music and records. The contents of the gramophone record collection are not, of course, confined to music. Speech records, such as poetry readings and Shakespearean and other plays, are available and are in great demand by users. Language tuition records are also very popular and need to be supplied in many duplicate sets. It is normal to issue the books published with speech and language records at the same time as the discs.

The gramophone record library calls for ancillary equipment, chief among which must be a good record player and amplifier so that records can be tested by the staff. A microscope for examining styli is another useful piece of equipment, and there are devices for cleaning LP records and ridding them of the static which accumulates on the plastic surfaces. Another consideration is the provision of special stationery needed for the issuing of records. Cardboard sleeves with printed date labels are of course a necessity, while some libraries issue their discs in protective cartons or boxes.

Where audio-visual departments do not exist, most gramophone record libraries are combined with the music department under the control of music librarians and a specialized staff. This enables users to have before them not only the stock of discs but also the whole of the music, including miniature scores, textbooks, reference books and periodicals. As previously mentioned, Scandinavian libraries began using records only for listening in the library, though many now lend as well. But the Scandinavian idea led to the wiring of the library, or part of it, for stereo, and to the provision of comfortable listening facilities in the library. Record players are operated from the service desk by the staff, but users can select their discs from the catalogue and sit comfortably in the library using earphones and controlling the volume themselves. It seems likely that most new British library buildings will in the future provide this facility in addition to loan privileges.

It should be mentioned that most gramophone record lending libraries issue discs to individual borrowers, though a few still restrict issues to societies only. The existence of a record library has also led some libraries to introduce lunch-hour concerts on their premises.

We have witnessed the development from standard play to long-playing records, and from monaural to stereo. Now we are seeing the advent of recorded cassettes and already some libraries are stocking these and issuing them to borrowers. It seems only a matter of time before cassettes become the normal media in this field.

REFERENCE AND LOCAL HISTORY LIBRARIES

Work in reference and local history libraries is becoming increasingly specialized, and it is not possible here to cover the subject in great detail. It should be mentioned at the outset that many libraries have abandoned the division between circulation and reference libraries, preferring to integrate the stocks and to arrange the collection in subject departments, all of which are staffed by subject specialists. Even in such arrangements, however, there are still many books for reference only and these are specially marked and may not be taken out on loan.

In systems where this integrated stock principle does not apply every library has its quick-reference section, ranging from a few shelves of reference books in small branch libraries to the important reference libraries of such cities as Glasgow and Manchester. The peculiar character of reference work, of course, is that of answering questions or providing information from books and other records for readers. For this reason, the book stock, staffing and routine methods of reference services differ considerably from those of other departments.

The medium-size reference service will contain dictionaries, encyclopaedias, directories, Government publications, bibliographies, atlases and maps, mathematical tables, yearbooks and similar material, backed by the recognized reference books on each subject. There will almost certainly be a local history collection, containing as much material as possible, whether it be books, manuscripts, maps, pictures, leaflets, programmes, illustrations, slides or other material relating to the locality.

In the largest library systems, the reference service contains textbooks on individual topics as well as all the general reference books already mentioned. It may grow to such proportions that, as at Manchester, separate technical, foreign and commercial libraries are set up or, as at Edinburgh and Liverpool, many subject departments are established on the integrated stock principle previously referred to.

The staffing of a reference and information service is a matter of the highest importance. The work calls for high degrees of bibliographical knowledge and experience, ingenuity and flexibility of mind, and the right psychological approach to enquirers. The latter is vitally significant for one of the most difficult tasks confronting a reference librarian is to get the enquirer to say exactly and specifically what information he is seeking. As a consequence, good reference librarians are among the most valuable members of any library staff.

Reference stock is rarely kept on the open shelves in its entirety, owing to its compass, also to the fact that much of it is of occasional use only, and finally because it may contain many books of a rare and irreplaceable nature. Usually only the best-known and most used reference books are kept on the open shelves, the remainder being readily accessible in book stores known as stacks. The whole stock, of course, will be represented in the catalogue, but those books not kept on open shelves should have their catalogue entries plainly marked to the effect that they are kept in reserve stock and are available on application to the staff. Access to open shelf stock will be without formality, but a simple form is normally used when the reader requires a particular book from the stack. What the staff should aim at here is speed in providing the book, as readers naturally find long waits irksome. Large reference libraries make use of pneumatic tubes and conveyor belts to improve their performance in providing books from the stack.

Reference libraries differ from other departments in their layout and furnishing, the best being fitted with flat study desks fitted with individual local lighting. Special attention is now being given to the needs of long-term research workers, and in an increasing number of libraries, study carrels are provided. At the end of his day's research, the student is issued with the key to the carrel so that he can lock it and begin work immediately next morning, having left his papers and books on the desk. Some libraries provide typewriters in their study carrels for the use of research workers. Some other libraries prefer to provide study rooms rather than individual carrels, rooms which have a number of desks, but here again the desks can be locked and students issued with keys for that purpose.

Special shelving is needed in reference libraries, since so many of the volumes are large in size, and there is also a need for special furniture in the way of map tables and cabinets, vertical or lateral files for keeping illustrations, cuttings and manuscripts. Microphotography has revolutionized reference work, and most reference services now have much microtext material, with the necessary microfilm, microfiche or microcard readers. Many files of newspapers and periodicals, as well as older volumes and documents, are now kept in microtext form. Finally, reprographic equipment is now an accepted part of most reference services, so that photocopies of written material can speedily and cheaply be provided for readers. An increasing number of libraries now have coin-operated photocopying machines in their public departments for this purpose. The alternative is for the library staff to carry out the photocopying work for readers on the library's own equipment and to make an economic charge for this.

PERIODICALS AND NEWSPAPERS

The provision of periodicals and newspapers in libraries calls for little complexity in the way of routines. Their arrival, of course, has to be checked on a register, and the visible index type is preferable to the inflexible ledger form. Invoices have to be checked, and the method of display has to be decided. The modern trend is to reduce the number of newspapers taken, but periodicals and journals remain a most important part of the library's information service.

Periodicals should be kept in cases with transparent fronts and lettered spines, and displayed on racks so that their titles can be clearly seen. Generous space should be allotted to periodicals when planning libraries, since both readers and librarians prefer to display them frontally. Apart from any other considerations, the variety and colour of periodicals' covers helps to improve the attractiveness of the library. Another matter calling for attention is the disposal of periodicals after use. Journals, particularly those on technical subjects, are of special value, and for this reason the majority are filed and often bound and added to the stock of the reference library. Decisions have to be made as to how long periodicals' files should be kept. It may be agreed, for example, to keep some ephemeral journals for only six months, one year or two years. Experience is the best teacher in arriving at these decisions.

Attention is drawn to the fact that the *Writers' and Artists' Year Book* contains a full list of current periodicals in the United Kingdom, as well as brief lists of those published in the United States and the Commonwealth. More specifically for librarians is the *Guide to Current British Journals*, compiled by D. Woodworth and published by the Library Association. A feature of this is the brief annotation which is offered under each title. Another useful guide, offering what amounts to an international guide is Ulrich's *Periodicals Directory*, an American publication. Two tools which are of great use to British librarians giving, as they do, details of the locations of periodicals' files, are the *British Union Catalogue of Periodicals* and the *London Union List of Periodicals*. Some large libraries also publish lists of their periodical holdings, an example being the *Westminster Union List of Periodicals*, issued by Westminster City Libraries.

Student librarians should handle as many good periodicals as they can, getting to know their format, scope and contents. The best periodicals are just as important as the best reference books.

CHILDREN'S LIBRARIES

Library service to children is of cardinal importance. Young people become adults in a relatively short time, and those who have enjoyed a good children's library service in their youth become better and more intelligent users of the adult library in later life. The children's library is usually a microcosm of the whole library as far as contents and methods are concerned. Normally occupying one room, it contains fiction and non-fiction books for home reading arranged in a similar manner to those in the adult library. It also has a reference collection which helps to familiarize children with the use of dictionaries, atlases, encyclopaedias and annuals, and it often supplies a range of children's periodicals.

A simplified version of the classification scheme is customary for the children's library, and the catalogue too is duly simplified. Registration is on similar lines to the system employed in the adult department, except that the signature of a parent or teacher is usually required on the application form. Age limits vary, but the contemporary tendency is to cater for all young people from the very youngest, and to have vitually no age restrictions. An increasing number of libraries have abolished charges for overdue books: in place of these, offenders are warned, and temporary suspension of borrowing privileges is sometimes applied to persistent offenders.

The staff of the children's library, particularly the qualified children's librarians, must be chosen with care. Special qualities are needed – patience, tact, sincerity and sociability – as well as organizing ability and a wide knowledge of children's literature and child psychology. The children's librarian is usually allowed a good measure of latitude in the running of her department. She does her own book selection, arranges displays, selects books for school libraries where these are provided, visits schools to give talks, receives school classes in the library, compiles printed or duplicated lists of new books, and generally endeavours to keep the children's library as attractive a place as possible.

Extension work is often undertaken in the way of book talks, story hours, library lessons and holiday activities. Story hours are arranged regularly, perhaps one or more a week being held in the children's library. Normally the story hour or book talk consists of the reading or telling of a story by the children's librarian or a member of her staff, but it should be remembered that narrative is a great art and a poor storyteller can ruin a good story. An experiment with tape recordings in the children's library proved to be a novelty accepted with enthusiasm by the young listeners. A story hour need not be confined to actual stories. Straight talks can be included, preferably illustrated with slides or film. One thing to bear in mind is that story hours should be related to the use of books: displays of relevant books or lists of recommended books should be a feature of them.

Special rooms for the story hour and other children's library activities are a feature of the best modern library buildings. Some very original conceptions of these can be seen in American and Scandinavian public libraries, and many British libraries have followed suit.

Children's book weeks have been popular and successful in many places. They usually consist of a programme of talks by well-known children's authors and illustrators, an exhibition of children's books past and present, and perhaps competitions for which book prizes are awarded. An essential factor in the success of a children's book week is the co-operation of schools and their teachers. Given that, the venture usually results in a noticeable improvement in the quality and quantity of children's reading.

Co-operation with schools and teachers is in any case a vital necessity in the success of children's library work generally. Fieldwork is frequently undertaken by the children's librarian who visits schools and addresses teachers and children on the work of the library. But a better idea is to arrange for classes to visit the library for a lesson on its facilities and use. A series of such visits could allow for the presentation of talks on the library as a whole, who owns it, where the money comes from, and how it is governed. Other talks could cover the care and handling of books, how to find books on the shelves, and how the catalogue can be used. Some practice could be given on the use of the catalogue and book-finding. Another period could be taken up by talking about reference books and demonstrating their use.

It must be remembered that such lessons need careful preparation in advance, especially when the children are themselves to be involved. Staff taking part must be carefully briefed and rehearsed so that the talks and demonstrations are properly stage-managed and supervised.

SERVICE TO YOUNG ADULTS

A hint was given earlier about having no age barriers to the use of children's libraries, and many children's librarians now supply books to nursery schools and play groups, as well as offering pre-school story hours. At the other end of the age scale come the young adults or teenagers, who have always posed a problem for librarians. It is unreasonable to expect young adults to continue using children's libraries, for they have reached the age when they want to cast off all connections with childhood.

The young adult finds many distractions to take his mind off books and reading, yet it is the period in his life when he is most impressionable and can get lasting value from the books he reads. Librarians have tried to retain the interest of young adults in several ways, chief among which is the provision of separate young adults' or teenagers' departments. Many examples exist in Scandinavia, Europe and the United States, but few in the United Kingdom. Such departments try to attract by offering a clublike atmosphere, with games such as chess, and record-listening facilities as well as the provision of books, newspapers and periodicals. The disadvantage of such rooms is their heavy cost, because they require additional staff and duplicate copies of books which may already be available in the adult library.

A great deal of professional literature has been written about the problem of young adults and their reading, but an accepted solution seems no nearer. Recent thought is veering away from separate young adults' departments, preferring to meet the problem by including specialist young adults' librarians on the staff. It will be interesting to see if this idea meets with any greater success.

Fortunately, this reluctance of young adults to use libraries seems to be a temporary phase only. When the distractions of study, TV, boy-friends and girl-friends have been experienced for a few years, most of those who previously used libraries as children return to make good use of them as adults. It seems as though the challenge of the young adults will be with librarians for some time to come and may never be completely and satisfactorily solved.

Chapter 8
Book Stock

Newcomers to the profession do not have the necessary experience to enable them to appreciate all the work involved before books are ready to be made available to readers. The purpose of this chapter is to outline these processes, through selection, ordering, processing and stock recording.

BOOK SELECTION

The selection of material for the library is a basic and important task and those responsible for it must have a wide knowledge of books, particularly in regard to present-day writers, and should also be endowed with the alert sense and necessary experience to enable them to assess potential public demand in advance. In the smallest libraries book selection is normally carried out by the chief librarian, although he should always be ready to welcome suggestions from readers and from his own staff. In larger libraries, the selection of materials is often decided by a committee of senior librarians, who collect requirements from all departments, including readers' requests, examine approval copies, and generally co-ordinate lists of approved additions. Sometimes, the head of the bibliographical section, who is often called a stock editor, is made responsible for co-ordinating selection.

Student librarians will find that there are different methods of selection in different libraries. Much depends on the size of a library or library system, and whether it is a general or a special library. One thing, however, should be appreciated from the outset, and that is that librarians should always resist the temptation to indulge in critical book selection. By this we mean the deliberate inclusion or exclusion of material which the librarian himself either likes or dislikes. It would be patently

wrong, for example, for a librarian to add an undue amount of
material on a topic in which he himself has a close interest, or to
deliberately exclude material on a subject which he personally
abominates, whether this be political, religious, ethical or any
other theme.

The true aim of a general library should be to present and
make freely available to readers all points of view on all topics,
so that people are given a fair opportunity of perusing all aspects
and making up their own minds. Censorship in any form should
be anathema to librarians. Many organizations, including
UNESCO, IFLA, the American Library Association, the (British)
Library Association, and similar bodies in other countries have
issued statements condemning censorship in libraries. Students
are referred to these, particularly the ALA Library Bill of
Rights, and André Maurios' *Public Libraries and their Mission*,
published by UNESCO.

SELECTION AIDS

Today there are many, probably too many, aids to the
selection of material, but it is never too early to become
acquainted with the best bibliographical and periodical aids.
For British librarians, whether they administer academic,
public or special libraries, the indispensable aid since 1950 has
been the *British National Bibliography*, which appears weekly,
and is cumulated quarterly and annually. Five-yearly cumulations of the index and of the subject catalogue are also published.
The BNB has been self-supporting and is governed by an *ad hoc*
body with representatives from the British Museum, Aslib, the
Library Association, the Publishers Association, the Booksellers Association and other bodies. As we have seen in
chapter 1, BNB will in future form part of the British Library.

The entries in BNB are based on the books which are legally
deposited by publishers under the Copyright Acts. For classification, it uses the Decimal scheme with many variations over
the years, but it is now basing its placings on the 18th and most
recent edition of the Decimal Classification. The entries are
fully catalogued according to the classified code, with author,
subject and title indexes.

Not only is BNB the weekly list on which librarians base their book selection, it also enables staff and readers to trace books from their authors or titles, and it facilitates the compilation of subject reading lists. It is not, of course, a complete guide to book selection, because it does not include music, maps or foreign books (except those which are published or are available in the United Kingdom), but it is still indispensable. For music, the Council of the BNB has, since 1957, been producing the *British Catalogue of Music*: this appears quarterly and its entries are arranged according to a specially compiled scheme of classification. This publication, too, is fully indexed and is cumulated annually.

Other aids to current book selection appear in such journals as *The Times Literary Supplement, The Times Educational Supplement, The Times Higher Educational Supplement*, the *Listener*, the *New Statesman, New Society*, the *Spectator*, the *Observer*, the *Sunday Times*, the *Sunday Telegraph, The Times*, the *Daily Telegraph* and the *Guardian*, all of which contain regular reviews of current general literature. Book selectors also use such special periodicals as *Nature* and the *New Scientist*, which both review scientific books, the *Musical Times*, which pays attention to books on music, the *Connoisseur*, which reviews art books, *Engineering*, which covers technical books, and many other journals covering many other specialist topics. There are also such aids as the *Bookseller* and the *Publishers' Circular*, both of which are trade publications appearing weekly and carrying lists of books published in the previous week as well as lists of forthcoming books. The special Spring and Autumn numbers of the *Bookseller* are of particular interest because of the detail they include about forthcoming publications.

Books and Bookmen is useful for its general reviews as well as for a list of forthcoming books, while a good reminder list is *Books of the Month*, which reviews and lists books published during the previous month. *British Book News*, issued by the British Council, is primarily intended for overseas readers, by whom it is regularly used for its reliability. It is well annotated and for this reason it is used as a checklist by many British librarians.

Basic bibliographical aids of which all students should be aware are the *Cumulative Book Index* or CBI, and *British Books in*

Print. The former is an American publication, a monthly list of new books in dictionary catalogue form, and cumulated into a bound volume every six months. Larger cumulations appear at longer intervals. Since 1930 the CBI has included not only American books but also those published in the United Kingdom and in other parts of the English-speaking world. This is one of its great merits. *British Books in Print* has evolved from a previous publication called the *Reference Catalogue of Current Literature,* and is issued in two volumes, one arranged alphabetically by authors, the other by titles. A parallel American publication is *Books in Print,* also in two volumes and published by R. R. Bowker.

There are, of course, many other aids to book selection and bibliographical tracing. These include the national biblio-graphies of various countries, catalogues of libraries such as the BML, the Library of Congress, the London Library, and an almost limitless number of subject guides and bibliographies issued by library associations, libraries, or individual compilers. These are mentioned only in passing at this stage: as he grows in experience the student librarian will use more of these in practice and will have to become familiar with the best of them for examination purposes.

BOOK ORDERING

The books having been selected, perhaps with the aid of some of the above guides, they have then to be ordered. Some purists in the profession have deplored the fact that, by and large, librarians have failed to evolve a systematic method of book selection. There is no need for such disparagement, for book selection does not always lend itself to rigid systematiza-tion. In book ordering, however, system is not only desirable, it is absolutely essential.

Methods differ from library to library, but the general method of recording book orders is to make out a card or slip for every book ordered and to file these in alphabetical order. The book order record will contain details of author, title, edition, publisher, price, date of order, from whom ordered, date of supply, allocation, accession number and Standard

Book Number. More and more libraries are computerizing their book ordering and cataloguing, and great economies are possible here since it is feasible at one typing to produce not only the order slip with copies but also the punched magnetic tape which can be forwarded to the computer centre as the catalogue entry.

In most libraries readers' requests are encouraged and these often form a considerable proportion of books on the order list. Such requests are made on a specially printed blank containing spaces for author, title, publisher, price, and the reader's name, address and telephone number. On the reverse can be printed details for office use only, such as whether the request is approved or rejected, whether the purchase will be made new or second-hand, or whether the request is to be met by borrowing through the co-operative interlibrary loan system. Readers' request cards are usually filed separately, each one being slipped in the book as it arrives. The card stays with the book through processing, and when the book is ready for issue, the reader is informed by post or telephone that the book is now available and that it is being reserved for him for a few days.

BOOK PROCESSING

At an early stage in their careers, student librarians should get to know the processes through which a book goes between its arrival from the bookseller and its appearance on the shelves of the library. This should be an easy matter for those who have worked in a library for a short time and have kept their eyes open. The stages of book preparation, or processing, can be tabulated as follows: check of book with invoice; rough collation (i.e. physical check of book to note any imperfections such as missing or duplicated sections); accessioning or stock recording; classification; cataloguing; lettering on spine; labelling; final check of all processes before shelving.

Now to examine these processes in a little more detail. As the new books are unpacked they are assembled for comparison with the invoice which the bookseller may either have included in the consignment or have sent under separate cover. Care must be taken to ensure that the correct prices have been charged, that the correct discount has been allowed, and the invoice must be checked for addition. Some libraries use a 'process-stamp' which is imprinted usually on the back of the title-page of each new addition, and this sometimes has spaces for filling in the vendor's name, price, date of addition and other details. The process-stamp, if used at all, should be kept as small and unobtrusive as possible. If a process-stamp is not in use, it will probably still be found necessary to write the accession number, the class number and the location of the book on the back of the title-page.

At the same time as the book is unpacked and checked with the invoice, it is advisable to carry out a quick check to make sure that the book has no physical imperfections. It sometimes happens that a book has been damaged in transit or that, owing to a binder's error, a section of the book is missing or has been duplicated. In the event of any such imperfections, the book will be returned to the bookseller, who will supply a perfect copy in its place. If he is unable to replace it, he will send a credit note, enabling the amount to be deducted from the full invoice before payment.

After these preliminaries the book (if non-fiction) will proceed to the classifier's desk or shelves for classification, and then it will be accessioned. Fiction will proceed directly to the accessions section immediately after being checked with the invoice. Here it should be mentioned that some libraries no longer accession fiction books. The various methods of accessioning will be more fully described later in this chapter. Following accessioning, the book proceeds to the cataloguer, although here again there are variations from library to library, especially where computerization is used in cataloguing.

The book is then released for its final processing, which includes stamping and labelling as well as lettering the class mark on the spine. This lettering is an important process and should preferably be done with a bookbinder's gold tooling set for greater permanence. If the lettering on the spine of a book becomes indecipherable, the last link in the whole chain of book tracing destroys the efficacy of the entire system. The whole object of classification and cataloguing, on which a formidable amount of time and money is spent in every library system, is to enable books to be grouped into the most useful order and to enable them to be easily found. If the lettering method is inefficient, then the whole book-finding system is inefficient and all the work that has gone into classification and cataloguing is wasted.

Before the book finally goes on to the shelves, a final check takes place. This is often done by a qualified librarian, who checks every process to make sure that none has been omitted and that all is in order.

STOCK RECORDING

The object of stock recording, or accessioning, is to show the history of any particular book from the time of its arrival in the library to the time of its withdrawal.

Stock records are usually called accessions registers and they may be in ledger, loose-leaf ledger, card, slip, punched card or magnetic tape form if the library is computerized. The information included in an accessions register usually comprises such details as accession number, author, title, publisher, date of publication, edition, price, vendor, class number, Standard Book Number, date of addition and allocation, that is, the department or branch to which the book has been allocated.

It is essential that accessions registers should be flexible in form, because most libraries have a high rate of turnover in regard to additions and withdrawals. Cards or slips have been in favour with most libraries, with one card or slip being completed for each book added to stock, these then being filed either in accession number order, class number order, or author order. When the book is withdrawn from the library, the accession card or slip can be destroyed and the vacant accession number used again for a new book or replacement. Some libraries keep records of withdrawn books, but there seems little justification for what is a useless and time-consuming record. Accuracy in maintaining the accessions register is essential at all times for it is regarded as the official stock record of the library. In case of fire, it should, along with the catalogue and the book issue records, be one of the first items to be taken to safety, as it may be required by the insurance company for assessing the value of the losses caused by the fire.

It must be emphasized again that in recent years libraries have made more and more use of computers, not only for cataloguing but for stock recording, book issuing and other processes. Where stock recording is on the computer, this is usually accepted by auditors as a reliable record, so that tangible accessions registers in the library cease to exist. The advent of Standard Book Numbers has also made it possible to avoid having separate accession numbers for each book. Instead, the SBN is used plus an identifying number for each individual copy of the book.

STOCKTAKING

Stocktaking is one of the most formidable tasks to be undertaken by the staff of any library, as it involves a physical check of each book in stock according to the accession records. In a library which is not open to the public, stocktaking is comparatively easy, but it is not so straightforward when the library is serving the public. Some authorities have been known to close their libraries for stocktaking, but such interference with a busy and much-used public service is difficult to justify. An alternative to stocktaking is to have a census of the books in the library. This count, deducted from the total number of books according to stock records, will show the number of books missing at the time of the count, but will not, of course, reveal the actual titles of missing books. For most libraries the days of annual stocktaking are over, owing to shortage of staff, but a useful idea is to compromise by having a stocktaking every five or seven years, with a simple census between each stocktaking. Another, and perhaps less painful way of tackling this thorny problem is to have a continual stocktaking over a library system as a whole, by checking first one library or department, then another.

Methods of stocktaking vary so much that it is impossible to describe them all. Much depends on the type of accessions records which are in use. The alert librarian, however, should always be alive to the need for using every modern aid. One possibility is to use an audio-method, using a small portable tape recorder with a lapel microphone. The recorded tapes can be played back later to a clerk who marks off details of the books checked against the accessions records. Computerized libraries may also find it possible to use other sophisticated aids, such as the Plessey pen method. The essential thing is to try to streamline this work to the utmost.

STATISTICS

Every student librarian should have an outline knowledge of the various statistics kept by his library, and the reasons for their maintenance. Most librarians have tended in the past to keep too many statistics and there has been much streamlining in this direction. But traditions die hard and it is still certain that unnecessary statistics are being maintained in many libraries. Every librarian should regard it as his urgent duty to keep only those statistics which have a positive and continuing use.

The essential records are those concerning stock, readers, and the use made of the library. For the first-named it is necessary to know the total stock, the number of books in each department or branch, and perhaps the number of books in each class, although the latter figures are now not regarded as essential. Statistics of readers sometimes include the number of tickets, but again this latter figure has been eschewed by most libraries.

Circulation statistics are kept by most libraries as a guide to their use. At one time some public libraries used to analyse the total circulation figures according to the main classes of the book classification used, but there has been a welcome trend to abandon such detail. Many librarians now maintain no more than a daily count of books loaned, and various labour-saving means of doing this have been evolved. Book loans in libraries which use photocharging, for example, are easily read off by referring to the serial numbers of the transaction cards used each day. Finally, most libraries keep ready figures of inter-library loans, both books borrowed and books lent.

Figures of the use of reference libraries are virtually impossible to maintain. There is no point in keeping statistics of books consulted because a knowledgeable reader or librarian may find the information he seeks from one book, whereas a less knowledgeable person may use six or ten books to elicit the same information. One can, however, keep figures of the number of readers who use reference libraries, and this could be done daily, though it is less troublesome and almost equally reliable to count the number of reference library users on selected days two or three times a year.

In these days when labour costs are so high it behoves every librarian to prune his statistics, and if he thinks he is keeping them for his governing body, he should ask that body if they really require the figures. It is strongly recommended that libraries should maintain only the following statistics:

(*a*) total stock, and stock of each department and branch;
(*b*) number of registered readers;
(*c*) departmental and branch circulation figures;
(*d*) books lent and borrowed through interlibrary loan systems.

Monthly and annual reports to library authorities have in the past been much too statistical. Both are more likely to succeed in their purpose when the figures are kept brief and are combined with lively comment on library trends and events. As far as the presentation of statistics in annual reports is concerned there is a good case for standardization as this aids comparison. The Library Association has a recommended form for the presentation of figures in annual reports of public libraries, and public librarians should adopt this wherever possible.

BINDING ROUTINE

A few larger libraries maintain home binderies, in which all or part of the book stock is rebound, reinforced or repaired as occasion arises. It is maintained by some of those librarians who have been operating home binderies for a long period that they are cheaper than using outside contractors. Be that as it may, it must be said that the work done by the recognized library binding contractors is generally very good, while the highly competitive prices tend to keep costs down. The clerical work connected with this is easily enough organized and carried out, but accuracy is of great importance, especially in the instructions given to the contractor as to the style and lettering of each book.

It is fairly general practice to type in duplicate the lists of books to be rebound, one copy going to the binder, the other being retained by the library. The details required are date of consignment; author and title in the form required for tooling on the spine; class number; and binding style. Libraries which send large consignments of fiction to outside binders usually request that they should be bound in assorted colours or styles. Non-fiction books require separate instructions, especially if some are important reference books to be bound for permanence in full, half or quarter leather. Lamination is a modern technique which has been used to good advantage by many libraries, and it is possible this way to bind the dust jacket or part of it with the covers, thus giving the impression of a new book and, incidentally, adding colour to the library shelves.

A number of European countries have what are known as library service agencies which centralize such processes as binding, the provision of catalogue cards and the production of co-operative bibliographies, booklists and library publicity. Examples of these are the Bibliotekstjänst for Sweden, the Biblioteksentralen for Norway, and an organization abbreviated as EKZ for West Germany. In agencies such as these, the tendency is for new books to be purchased direct from the publishers in sheets, then the sheets are bound for library use and the books are retailed to libraries through designated booksellers. The Bibliotekstjänst (or Library Service) in Sweden has proved conclusively that this is cheaper than each library arranging its own binding, and the library service agencies in other countries where they operate would no doubt confirm this.

CARE OF BOOKS

While on the subject of binding, a few words may perhaps be added on the care of books generally. Standards of book handling and book care have deteriorated recently, and library personnel are as much to blame as the public – perhaps more so, because they should know better. Because books belong to a library which is communally owned, there is no reason why they should be treated with the vandalism which they sometimes are. There is room for great improvement in the handling of books by library staffs, and one can only hope that the care of books will soon re-assume its rightful place as an important aspect of library science.

The advent some years ago of plastic book jackets has been an important factor in maintaining the attractiveness of new books and in helping to prolong their lives. Readers appreciate the fact that the plastic jackets preserve the original dust-jackets of books, and such jackets have a good psychological effect upon readers, who tend to handle with more care books which appear to be in good condition. There can be few libraries which do not now make use of plastic jackets, which can be fitted either by specialist contractors or by personnel in the library.

Reinforced bindings are another factor in the struggle to maintain attractive books on library shelves. These have been introduced by a number of library binding contractors. By arrangement with various publishers they buy the sheets of selected new books and reprints, and bind these for libraries in attractive and reinforced bindings. Children's books especially lend themselves to this treatment, and the idea, whether applied to children's or to adult books, is one that has been warmly appreciated by both readers and librarians.

OFFICE MANAGEMENT

This chapter is concluded with a very short description of office routine as applied to libraries, because few student librarians have the opportunity of becoming acquainted with this aspect in a practical way. In the smallest libraries, one member of the staff is usually earmarked for clerical work, perhaps in addition to normal library duties. In larger services, more full-time clerical assistants will be needed, while in the biggest systems a separate administrative section is needed to keep up with the essential clerical and office work. The chief duties involved in library office work are:

(*a*) typing and filing of correspondence;

(*b*) typing and duplicating of committee reports, booklists, lecture programmes, exhibition catalogues and other material;

(*c*) maintenance of postage accounts, petty cash accounts, order books and other records;

(*d*) check of goods with invoices, check of invoices and statements, preparation of invoices for certification and payment, and maintenance of expenditure books;

(*e*) maintenance of receipt books and paying-in of cash receipts;

(*f*) check of stationery items and re-ordering of essential supplies;

(*g*) maintenance of staff records, including records of annual leave, special leave, and sickness records;

(*h*) preparation of wages-sheets for employees;

(*i*) maintenance of up-to-date catalogues of furniture and equipment, as well as the inventory of furniture and equipment held.

The typing and filing of correspondence is an important and responsible duty. The librarian should insist on a fixed style of typing, so that all correspondence leaving his library conforms to a neat and legible pattern. With every outgoing letter there should be a carbon copy and this should be filed with a letter, if any, to which it is a reply. The usual method of filing papers is to use manila folders in vertical or lateral files. As far as the arrangement of the folders is concerned, there are several alternative methods, and each librarian will choose that which is most convenient for his own use. One way is to arrange them alphabetically by correspondent, but this has the disadvantage of separating papers relating to the same subject, and a subject index would be necessary. Alternatively, the arrangement can be alphabetical by subjects, but here an index of correspondents would be needed. A third method is to combine the two systems previously mentioned, and to have an alphabetical arrangement of both subjects and correspondents. This frequently results in cross-classification, but is a good rough-and-ready arrangement for small libraries.

The fourth, and probably the best method, is to classify the papers systematically according to some published scheme, such as the schedules 020 to 029 in the Decimal Classification, or according to J. D. Stewart's *Tabulation of Librarianship*. The latter has proved to be an effective scheme, and has been put into operation in a number of libraries. Whatever systematic arrangement is used, an index of correspondents should be maintained.

Any good book describing the elements of office routine will give the student useful information on simple book-keeping, such as the maintenance of postage books, petty cash account books, and receipt and expenditure books. A few words should perhaps be added on the use of order books. These are generally used by government departments, universities, local authorities and industrial organizations, and the most usual kind provide for the recording of orders in triplicate. The original is sent to the vendor, the second copy is attached to the invoice after the goods have arrived, and the two are sent to the finance department, while the third and last copy remains in the order book as a record.

Those engaged in administrative work today have to become familiar with the use of machinery and equipment such as electric typewriters, duplicators, photocopying machines, telex, postal franking machines and other office hardware. Some of these are hired from contractors and are serviced by them. Such arrangements involve initial agreements which should be read most carefully before being signed.

Enough has been said to convey the idea that no library service can be efficient unless it is backed by a sound and well-managed administrative machine. The administrative section must work closely with other departments of the authority, in relation to legal and financial matters, in connection with staff establishment work, and also in relation to the care and maintenance of buildings, furniture and equipment. Meticulous filing and keeping of records is called for, especially in connection with expenditure on books, binding, periodicals, gramophone records, travel expenses and other items of the budget. Particular stress must be laid on control of book expenditure, for the librarian often requires details of the up-to-date position, and these must be supplied by the administrative section of the library.

Chapter 9
Elements of classification and cataloguing

Classification is the process by which we group things according to their likenesses and separate them according to their differences. In everyday life this process is almost automatic, because we classify things unconsciously in our thoughts every time we use an adjective. When we think of the term 'cat' we automatically exclude from our minds every other kind of animal. But if we go further and think of 'a black cat' we narrow our field, excluding from our grouping all cats which are not black. We carry the grouping process further still when we say 'a big black cat', the additional adjective helping to class the type more specifically, separating it from all small black cats.

The object of classification is to arrange things in the most helpful order for the purpose in hand. Note the word 'helpful', for convenience is the deciding factor which should govern the particular way in which things are classified. It will be perfectly obvious that the same things can be classified in different ways by different people for different purposes. It does not necessarily follow that one way is right and another way is wrong, for everything depends upon the purpose for which the classification is being made. The bank teller who arranges coins in piles according to their value is doing so because it suits his convenience in reckoning them. A numismatist, on the other hand, may be found arranging them in historical order. In each case the arrangement is the most suitable one for the purpose in hand.

Examples of classification in everyday life abound. For instance, in a tobacconist's shop the cigarettes are arranged by make, because it is by the brand that the customer asks for them. In a general store, commodities are arranged separately so that the shopkeeper can go straight to the shelves containing sugar or coffee or tea when he is asked for these things.

BOOK CLASSIFICATION

As far as books are concerned, it must be obvious that there are many possible ways of arranging them, either by size, by press, by publisher, colour of binding, alphabetically by subject, alphabetically by author, or by systematic subject arrangement. In the early days of libraries, books were grouped, arranged or classified by all these methods, and probably in other ways as well, but it was eventually discovered that the most convenient characteristic, or way of arranging books, was to group them systematically by subject. This method, by the way, has been found to be the best for both readers and librarians. Consequently a number of schemes of book classification were evolved by librarians: these have been published in book form and have been used in practice by various libraries.

Chief among these book or bibliographical schemes is the Decimal Classification. This was formulated by Melvil Dewey, an American librarian, in 1876, and it is now in its 18th edition. The early editions were relatively simple but, as time went on, the subdivisions were carried further and further until the 14th edition, which appeared in 1942, represented a summit in the scheme's development. All this expansion had taken place without any re-allocation of the original classes and main divisions, and it became increasingly clear that the proportions of the scheme were becoming ill-balanced and out-of-date.

Drastic changes were decided upon, and in 1951 there appeared the 15th (Standard) edition. These much briefer schedules were compiled by the staff of the Library of Congress in Washington, and show the influence of the Library of Congress's own scheme. This edition was, however, criticized as being altogether too lacking in detail, and the 16th, 17th and 18th editions have tended towards greater subdivisions of the schedules. Despite its many faults, the Decimal Classification is the most popular scheme in the English-speaking world, a large majority of libraries in the United Kingdom and the United States using it. DC, as it is known, is used by the *British National Bibliography* for its classified arrangement, and it also formed the basis of the Universal Decimal Classification, mentioned later in this chapter. DC has also been adapted by some foreign countries, an example being Denmark, where the national scheme is DC-based, though with some salient alterations from the original.

Another important classification scheme is that of the Library of Congress (LC) which was formulated in outline in 1899 by Herbert Putnam. It has since been greatly expanded and each class is now published separately. This scheme was specially prepared for use in the Library of Congress itself, and since this was, and is, a huge collection on the national and international scale, special problems were presented which the classification scheme tried to accommodate. For this reason the LC scheme was not originally advanced as a classification to be adopted by other libraries. Nevertheless it was used elsewhere, in the United Kingdom by the National Library of Wales and the Edinburgh Public Libraries. In recent years many large American university and public libraries have been changing from DC to LC to ensure more compatibility with the MARC (machine readable cataloguing) tapes being produced by the Library of Congress.

The Universal Decimal Classification (UDC) is an expansion of the Dewey scheme, and it was evolved at Brussels in 1895. As its name suggests, it was an attempt to make the Decimal Classification more applicable to the world in general, and to extend it so that it could be used for arranging not only books but MSS., cuttings, prints, pictures, slides and other material. The UDC should not be regarded as a mere extension of the Decimal Classification, because it is to all intents and purposes a separate scheme with many different features. Its auxiliary signs, which are additional to the DC notation, should be particularly studied. Abridgements of the UDC scheme in English are published by the British Standards Institution.

One of the most interesting published schemes is the Colon Classification of S. R. Ranganathan, published at Madras in 1933. Ranganathan saw problems in book arrangement which were not fully solved by the enumerative schemes such as DC, and his own scheme is not a hierarchical list of subjects.Instead he provides the classifier with the means of building together his own class number, and it is his claim that every book, however minute and specialized its topic might be, can be given a specific number in the Colon scheme. Much original thought

9

went into the preparation of this scheme and it has many novel features. Although it has not been put into practice in a general British library, it has influenced many classifiers, particularly those associated with BNB, and it has had a distinct influence upon a number of schemes devised to arrange special subjects. An example is the scheme specially prepared for the *British Catalogue of Music*. This special classification scheme was issued in 1960.

The latest of the general book schemes to be published is the Bibliographical Classification of Henry Evelyn Bliss, issued in New York from 1935 onwards, and finally completed in four volumes by 1953. This was formulated by Bliss for use in his own library, that of the City College of New York. He began work on it as early as 1903 and its completion was the result of a lifetime's study of the organization of knowledge as presented in book form. The scheme has had a number of adherents in the United Kingdom and a few special libraries use parts of the scheme for arranging their contents. They are greatly helped by the issue of a bulletin published by the H. W. Wilson Co. which helps to keep the scheme up-to-date for users.

Two other general schemes of book classification were described in earlier editions of this book, but both are now mainly of historical interest. One was the Expansive Classification of C. A. Cutter published in Boston, Mass., in 1891, and the other was the Subject Classification of James Duff Brown, the celebrated British librarian. This was first published in 1906, with a second edition in 1914. A third edition, brought up-to-date by J. D. Stewart, who was Brown's nephew, appeared in 1939. Many British public libraries adopted the Subject Classification, preferring its British approach to the American slant of DC, but over the years it gradually lost favour, and most of these public libraries have now reverted to DC.

SPECIAL FEATURES OF BOOK CLASSIFICATION

As readers will have gathered, a printed classification for arranging books is called a scheme. The schedules are the headings which comprise the scheme. In addition to the schedules, systems of book classification include certain auxiliaries such as a generalia class, form classes, form divisions, a notation and an index. These are now explained, with special reference to the Decimal Classification.

A Generalia class is a special feature designed to accommodate such works as encyclopaedias, general periodicals and newspapers, and other types of books which cover knowledge in general. Although the contents of most generalia classes are indeed general subjects, some schemes include here subjects considered to be pervasive of other classes. For example, in the Subject Classification of Brown, mathematics and logic are included in Generalia, while in the Decimal Classification the inclusion of bibliography will be noted.

Generalia classes are usually considered to be form classes, that is, a class of books grouped by the form in which they are written and presented. The Decimal Classification's Generalia class is more accurately described as a mixture of a form and a subject class, because in addition to encyclopaedias, essays, periodicals, bibliographies and newspapers, which are forms, it also contains actual subjects such as librarianship, museums and journalism.

The usual form class in a book classification is the Literature class, which includes poetry, drama, fiction, essays, speeches and letters. The Literature class in the Decimal Classification is numbered 800 to 899. In this, Dewey divides first by language, e.g. English, German, French, and then by form, e.g. poetry, drama, fiction and so on. Even though the 800 class of DC appears to be completely a form class, it is again to some small extent a mixture of subject and form, because it includes, and rightly so, books about the various forms as well as books written in those forms. For instance, the English poetry schedules will accommodate not only Browning's poetry but also books about that poetry.

Form divisions are really the generalia of each specific subject. It will be obvious that any subject may be presented in books in different forms, say in essay or in encyclopaedia form, or from different aspects, such as the historical or philosophical standpoint. Recognizing this, the formulators of the chief bibliographic schemes have added these so-called form divisions to the schedules of their schemes. In DC these are known as common form subdivisions, because they may be applied to most, though not quite all, parts of the schedules. These common form subdivisions in DC are nine in number, examples being 01 for philosophy, and 09 for history. A book on the philosophy of history is classed at 901, and one on the history of philosophy at 109. The number for English drama is 822, and a book on the history of English drama would go at 822.09.

A notation consists of the symbols adopted by a book classification to signify the classes, divisions and subdivisions which form the schedules. A notation may be pure or mixed, a pure notation being one in which only one kind of symbol is used, and a mixed notation being one in which two or more kinds of symbols are utilized. The DC notation is pure, as figures only are used, while the LC notation is mixed, because both letters and figures form the notation. The essential qualities of a notation are that it should be brief, simple, flexible and easy to say, write, read and understand. It should also convey as much as possible the order of the schedules. It does not matter whether a notation is pure or mixed, so long as it satisfies most or all of these conditions.

Some schemes feature mnemonics in their notation. A mnemonic is a memory-aiding device and it is in the Decimal Classification that we find mnemonics most skilfully used. The form divisions, because they are common throughout nearly the whole scheme, acquire a mnemonic value because they are so often in use. Another DC memory-aid is the system of geographical subdivisions. At frequent points in the scheme we find the instruction: 'Divide like 940–999'. For example, at 581.9 this is found, enabling a book on the flora of Wales to be classed at 581.9429, the 429 being the geographical number for Wales derived from 942.9. A further example of DC mnemonics is the planned similarity in the Language and Literature classes. For instance, 430 is German language and 830 is German literature, while 460 is Spanish language and 860 Spanish literature. The 3 is derived from 943, History of Germany, and the 6 comes from 946, History of Spain.

An index is an alphabetical list of the terms or names used in the schedules, giving the notation for each term. It is an essential without which no book classification is complete. In DC a relative index is used, and this is one which lists each subject in all its relations with other subjects. A glance at the Relative Index of DC will reveal its completeness and utility. To conclude this section on book classification here, in brief, are the essentials of a good bibliographical scheme. It should be complete, covering all branches of knowledge, and it should be kept up-to-date by frequent revisions. If possible, a bulletin should be published giving decisions and placings for new subjects. This is done for the Bliss scheme, and also for DC since the appearance of the 16th edition. Schemes should also be systematic, proceeding from the simple to the complex, and the terms used in them should be clear and comprehensive. A good scheme should be printed in convenient form and it ought to be flexible and expansible. Finally, it should include, as we have just seen, generalia and form classes, form divisions, a suitable notation and a relative index.

CLASSIFICATION RESEARCH

In recent years a great deal of research has been undertaken and is still going on in the fields of classification, information retrieval and data processing. This followed the publication of the schemes of Bliss and Ranganathan, and there is now general acceptance of the view that there are definite limitations in the basic structure of enumerative book classification schemes. The growth of literature, particularly in the scientific and technological areas, has outpaced the standard schemes and the gap between bibliographical requirements and the schedules of the traditional classifications is widening rapidly. Further, the subject matter of books is more frequently a combination of several elements and aspects, and it is considered better to represent these by assembling numbers from special tables rather than by attempting to enumerate every possible topic.

An important factor in the revival of interest in classification has been the development of mechanical or electronic information retrieval, and the application of computers to literature searching. British librarians have played a leading part in these studies and in 1952 a Classification Research Group was formed in Britain. Consideration of its work is the province of more advanced students than those for whom this book is intended, but it is important that they should know of the existence of this Group. Its members have written many original papers and articles, while the Group as a whole issues a bulletin and sponsored *The Sayers Memorial Volume,* a book published by the Library Association in 1961 to commemorate the work done for librarianship and classification by W. C. Berwick Sayers. It should be noted that there is also a classification research group in the United States and Canada.

The future of book classification seems now to be inextricably linked with the development of machine systems, and we may yet witness the decline of the enumerative schemes at present in use in favour of a new scheme designed for use with computerization. R. E. Coward has categorically stated that 'there is one thing that can be said with certainty about the DC and LC classifications. They are totally unsuitable for machine systems. This might turn out to be a good thing. The field is open for a general classification designed for use with computer systems. If one were developed now there is a good chance that it could become established.'

PRACTICAL ASPECTS OF BOOK CLASSIFICATION

Elementary problems of shelf arrangement, guiding and display work are the concern of every librarian, and these practical aspects of book classification must now be mentioned in a little more detail. Once books are classified according to a recognized scheme, it would appear that the obvious order in which to shelve them would be strictly according to the notation, and in one sequence only. One does not have to work long in a library however, to realize that practical considerations preclude this. Fiction, for example, is stocked in such numbers that, if it were classed at 823 (assuming the Decimal Classification to be in use), it would dislocate the whole scheme of arrangement if all novels were shelved at that number. Most libraries, therefore, treat fiction entirely separately and arrange it on the shelves in alphabetical order by authors' names.

Music too, on account of its size, demands a different type of shelving from that normally used for books, and this means that it cannot necessarily be shelved between the photography books of 770–779 and the sports and pastimes books of 790–799. Indeed, since the advent of collections of gramophone records and cassettes, many library authorities have formed an entirely separate department for music and records, often with listening facilities for students.

In addition, in nearly every class there are oversized books such as quartos and folios which demand special shelving and arrangement. The commonest treatment for oversized books is to shelve them altogether in an entirely separate sequence from 000 to 999, though some libraries prefer to shelve the oversized books of each main class separately at the end of each class. Indeed, the number and incidence of such books is increasing so rapidly that this latter idea is probably preferable. The catalogue entries for these books must be marked in a distinctive way so that readers wanting any of them will be directed to the shelves for oversized books.

Special collections, such as bequests of books on a particular subject, often have to be kept as separate entities because of the terms of the bequest, and this is another factor which may lead to an additional sequence. Finally, shelf arrangement may be affected by displays of books on certain subjects which the library may arrange from time to time. Books forming part of a display will be taken out of their correct classified sequence and located together on special shelves, book troughs or display tables. This is called broken order, but it should be noted that the shelving of oversized books in a separate sequence of the scheme is not broken order so much as a parallel arrangement.

One of the most vital practical aspects of book classification is that of guiding the library. A library without guides is like a road system without signposts. The guides usually provided are the catalogue; a plan of the library prominently displayed; class guides printed at the end of each bookcase; shelf guides; class-numbers lettered on the spines of books; a personal guide or library host for new readers; a readers' adviser on duty at all times; and a printed pamphlet describing the use of the catalogue and including a brief explanation of the classification scheme and the shelf arrangement.

The most important of these is the personal guide or library host. Very often this job is done by the readers' adviser.

Personal experience teaches us that there are so many posters and placards in modern life that people generally are becoming immune to printed advice and directions. Essential though shelf labels and printed guides might be, people take more notice of oral guidance and this is where the personal guide is useful. An increasing number of libraries have successfully instituted the practice of personally showing round new readers, and explaining the system of book arrangement to them. The library host or hostess should become a permanent feature in all large libraries.

CLASSIFICATION AND ITS RELATION TO CATALOGUING

Classification and cataloguing are complementary because they are both aids which librarians have devised to help readers find the books and information they are seeking. The essential difference between classification and cataloguing is that whereas in classification a book may be located at only one place on the shelves, in the catalogue it may be represented in several places. For example, a book treating equally of architecture, sculpture, painting and engraving presents a problem to the classifier. He can give it only one placing: shall he place it with the books on architecture, with those on painting, with those on sculpture, or with those on engraving? There is a fifth possibility: shall he regard it as a book on art in general and place it with the general books on the fine arts? Whatever decision he arrives at, the classifier should be guided by the law of convenience, in other words he should place the book where it will be most useful to the majority of readers.

The cataloguer has no such problem: dealing as he does with entries rather than a physical book, he can represent the book under each of its subjects, so that the students of architecture, engraving, painting and sculpture will, on consulting the catalogue, be informed of the book's presence and place in the library. In this way, therefore, are classification and cataloguing complementary and of mutual assistance to each other.

ELEMENTS OF CATALOGUING

It is now time to deal with the elements of cataloguing, and to begin by asserting that a catalogue is an essential tool in any library, as necessary as a town plan in a guidebook or as an index in a book. It is essential not only to the readers who use the library, but also to the staff who administer it. Without an efficient, up-to-date catalogue the staff cannot tell readers what books there are in the library, they cannot demonstrate to readers the library's resources on any given subject, and they lack a ready guide to the library's strengths and weaknesses. This latter facility is obviously one of the most vital needs in book selection.

The purposes of a library catalogue may be summarized as follows:

(*a*) to show what books the library possesses by a certain author;

(*b*) to show the stock of the library on any given subject;

(*c*) to show whether the library has a book bearing a certain title;

(*d*) to show, on each entry, such bibliographical information as date of publication, edition, whether the book is illustrated or contains maps or plans, its size and its pagination. The entry will also contain the accession number of the book and a reference to its location, i.e. its class-number and the particular library where it is in stock.

The chief types of library catalogue are the author, the dictionary, the classified, and the alphabetical-classed catalogues. The author catalogue speaks for itself, being simply a list of the books in the library arranged by their authors' names. It is rarely, if ever, used alone, and it need not concern us here. Neither need the alphabetical-classed catalogue, which is also uncommon nowadays. In this, books were arranged under their subjects, and the subject-headings were then listed in alphabetical order. Later in this chapter the dictionary and the classified catalogues will be mentioned at greater length.

TYPES OF CATALOGUES

At the beginning of the present century there was a vogue for producing complete printed catalogues of libraries, especially for public libraries, but this was for the good reason that most libraries were on closed access, working on the indicator system, and printed catalogues were almost essential. As more public libraries began to operate open access, printed catalogues became less necessary and their disadvantages became more apparent. They were costly and laborious to produce, and they were also out-of-date long before they appeared and could be kept current only by the issue of frequent supplements.

Libraries then went over to the more flexible types of catalogue, either on cards or slips, both of which were easily manœuvrable. However, as library systems grew in size, the disadvantages of both the card and the sheaf catalogue manifested themselves. They proved to be heavy on stationery, and on the necessary furniture, especially the bulky card catalogue cabinets. They were also costly in terms of staff time, especially in systems with branches where union catalogues were maintained.

With the advent of computers, librarians both in the United States and in the United Kingdom saw the advantages that would accrue from producing library catalogues with their aid. In the early 1960s experiments were taking place towards this end, and by the middle of that decade many librarians were ready to computerize their catalogue production. In the United Kingdom, some of the Greater London boroughs and the county libraries led the way. The immediate advantages of the computer catalogue are that additions and withdrawals can be reflected in the next print-out, and that, with photocopying of print-outs, every branch in the library complex can have a copy and can thus give a prompter service to readers. With the old card catalogues it had become usual to maintain a union catalogue showing locations at the main library, leaving the branch libraries only with catalogues of their own book stocks. This meant a constant relay of enquiries from branches to the main library asking for locations of books in the system.

Where catalogues are produced by the computer, every

branch and service point can be equipped with a copy of the union catalogue showing locations, thus reducing the enquiry traffic to a minimum. A recent development is to abandon the photocopying of print-outs and instead to reproduce them on microfilm. This means having microfilm readers with the catalogue cassettes in the public departments of libraries for readers' use, which sounds costly, but it can be demonstrated that, in the long term, this method is cheaper than photocopying. This Computer Output Microfilm (com) method has also proved acceptable to readers, most of whom use it without undue difficulty.

THE DICTIONARY CATALOGUE

This has been a very popular form of library catalogue for general public libraries, and has been particularly favoured in the United States. It is called a dictionary catalogue because the entries, consisting of author entries, subject entries, cross-references and title entries, are arranged in one alphabetical sequence like a dictionary. In a dictionary catalogue the main entry for all books (except anonymous works) is the author entry. Added entries usually appear under the subject or subjects treated by the book, and under the title if the subject is not implicit in the title.

The main entry is usually the only one containing a full description of the book, and added entries are often shortened and do not contain the same full bibliographical details. The popularity of the dictionary catalogue for general public libraries is due to the fact that its arrangement and use is easily explained to readers. The simple requirements of general readers are usually for books by a certain author, books on a stated subject, or a book with a particular title, and it is simple to demonstrate to readers that in the dictionary catalogue all these entries are sorted into one alphabetical arrangement.

Unfortunately, the dictionary catalogue also has numerous disadvantages. It is frowned upon because the use or misuse of subject headings can easily lead to inconsistency, confusion and chaos in the hands of inexpert cataloguers. An inexorable rule of dictionary cataloguing is that subject entries for books must be made under the names of the *specific* subjects treated by those books, and that references must always be made from the *general* to the *specific* and not vice versa. A book on Rome would for example be entered under ROME and not under ITALY. But there would have to be a cross-reference from ITALY and most libraries using the dictionary catalogue would use a reference as follows:

> ITALY
> *See also* under names of individual provinces and cities, e.g. LOMBARDY, ROME, etc.

A reference of this kind, once made, can be left in the catalogue and needs no additions. Even though it leaves readers wanting books on specific parts of the subject to search under the names of the specific subjects themselves it is a quite effective form of reference. It is because of the difficulties which can arise from subject entries and cross-references that confusion can occur in dictionary catalogues, and these problems, coupled with the fact that the dictionary form does not readily show the relationships between subjects, have prejudiced many librarians against its use.

One answer to these difficulties is to provide cataloguers with a set list of subject-headings and references. American librarians discovered this need a long time ago, and there are in existence several printed lists of subject-headings for use in dictionary catalogues, notably the *ALA List of Subject Headings for Use in a Dictionary Catalog*.

Librarians using the dictionary form often compile their own lists of subject-headings, basing them on one of the printed lists and making due allowance for differences between American and English terminology and spelling. The obvious advantages of having a list of subject-headings on the desk of the dictionary cataloguer are that it saves time and many excursions to the actual catalogue, and that it makes for uniformity, so that a succession of cataloguers can, if necessary, be employed without adversely affecting the uniformity and accuracy of the catalogue as far as the subject-headings are concerned.

THE CLASSIFIED CATALOGUE

The popularity of the classified catalogue in British libraries, public, special and academic, has been widespread, and when the *British National Bibliography* began publication in 1950 the fact that it was in classified form was taken for granted by British librarians. Its annual volumes provide student librarians with excellent opportunities of studying a fine example of the classified catalogue, with author and subject indexes. Furthermore, the example of BNB has converted a number of British libraries to this form, with the result that the classified catalogue has now more adherents than ever before.

The classified catalogue is undoubtedly easier for cataloguers to keep in order, but on the other hand it is not so easy to explain to the general reader. Nevertheless, in the long run, readers themselves stand to benefit more from the classified rather than the dictionary form, and for larger public libraries, for special and academic libraries, and indeed for all collections which are pre-eminently used by more serious readers, the classified catalogue supported by author and subject indexes is undoubtedly to be preferred. Recent increases in the student population have meant greater demands on libraries from readers who generally make a subject-approach to books, and this factor also has strengthened the claims for the classified catalogue as against the dictionary form.

But what is a classified catalogue? It is one in which the main entries are arranged in the same order as the classification scheme in use or, if you like, according to the order in which the books are arranged on the shelves. The heading, or arranging factor, of each entry is not the author or the name of the subject, as in the case of the dictionary catalogue, but the class-number itself.

This mode of arrangement means, of course, that it is impossible for anyone to understand the sequence of the entries unless they are familiar with the classification scheme in use. Very few readers are, in fact, familiar with library classification so that the main classified catalogue remains more or less a staff tool. Further aids to readers are, however, provided in the shape of separate author and subject indexes. These, especially the author index, are more heavily used by readers than the main catalogue.

The main entry, that is the one in the main catalogue, is of course the most complete entry. The author index entry usually contains little more than the author's name, the title of the book, its date and class-number, while the subject index entry contains merely the name of the subject and a straight reference to the class-number for that subject. In the main entry the class-number is prominently placed because all entries in the main catalogue are arranged according to that number or symbol.

The outstanding advantage of the classified catalogue is that all related subjects appear together, which means that the library's resources on a particular subject can easily be ascertained. If a reader who is interested in gardening consults the classified catalogue under the class symbol for that subject he has before him a conspectus of the library's holdings not only on gardening generally but also in all the specific aspects of the subject. If the same reader were to consult a dictionary catalogue he would presumably look first under GARDENING and at the end of the entries under that heading he would find references directing him to a large number of specific subjects which might involve him in many further consultations at various places in the alphabetical sequence. Thus, by affording a subject-survey of the stock, and for ease in assisting the staff in the compilation of subject lists, the classified catalogue has an over-riding advantage over the dictionary form.

Whichever form of catalogue is used, it is essential that the cataloguing should be accurate and consistent, and that adequate written guides are available directing readers how to use the catalogues.

As far as guides are concerned, the reader cannot have too many of these. Whether the catalogue be on cards, slips, printed or in microform, detailed directions as to its use, with examples, should be provided in all public departments. Many libraries issue new readers with folders on the resources and use of their collections, and this ought certainly to contain paragraphs on the understanding of the catalogue. Examples should be given copiously, for most readers can grasp these more quickly than they can understand detailed directions.

MAIN AND ADDED ENTRIES

The difference between main and added entries should already be apparent. In a dictionary catalogue the main entry is generally, though not always, the author entry. In the case of an anonymous book, entry is made under the title, and this then becomes the main entry. Added entries will be made under subjects, forms, series and sometimes under the title. In a classified catalogue the main entry is the subject entry, with the class symbol as the arranging factor. The author and subject index entries become the added entries, while other added entries may appear in the form of references and analytical entries.

REFERENCES

Little difficulty should be experienced in regard to the difference between *See* and *See also* references. A *See* reference is one which is made from a heading under which there are no other entries, to a heading which contains other entries. When it is desired to refer from a heading which already contains other entries to another heading, then a *See also* reference is used.

CODES OF CATALOGUING

It cannot be stressed too frequently that accuracy and uniformity are the prerequisites of good cataloguing, and we have already noted that as far as subject-headings for a dictionary catalogue are concerned it is essential to have an agreed list which the cataloguer can use as a constant guide. But what about the technical process of cataloguing itself? How are we to ensure uniformity in the matter of making catalogue entries? It will be immediately obvious that there can be many ways of making entries, and that when the cataloguer is faced with books written by joint authors, by those with hyphenated names, by noblemen, by married women, pseudonymous and anonymous writers, corporate authors and many other varieties of authorship and editorship, decisions must be made to ensure consistency of treatment. These decisions, when gathered together with examples, are known as cataloguing codes. There are many cataloguing codes in existence all over the world, but in the English-speaking countries there are three well-known ones. These are:

C. A. Cutter's *Rules for a Dictionary Catalog*, first published in the United States in 1876.

The British Museum's *Rules for Compiling the Catalogues in the Department of Printed Books*, which first appeared in 1839.

The *Anglo-American Joint Cataloguing Code*, compiled by committees of the Library Association and the American Library Association, which was first published in 1908, but appeared in a revised edition in 1967.

The most important and widely used of the above codes is the Anglo-American one. Co-operation between the two associations was renewed in 1936 with the intention of preparing a new edition, but war intervened and it was not until 1951 that the collaborative moves were resumed. In the meantime, the American Library Association had in 1949 independently produced and published the *ALA Cataloguing Rules for Author and Title Entries*.

For a number of years there were many meetings on both sides of the Atlantic and, in addition to the American and British associations, there were significant contributions from the Canadian Library Association and the Library of Congress. The basis of the present edition was the Paris Principles of the International Conference on Cataloguing Principles adopted in 1961. Owing to the different conditions in North America and Great Britain, complete accord was perhaps not to be expected, and neither was it attained. Nevertheless, there was a large measure of agreement. In the event, it was decided to publish two separate editions, a North American text and a British text.

The British text of *Anglo-American Cataloguing Rules* (AACR), as it is now called, was published by the Library Association in 1967. Comparison with the volume of 1908 shows that it is a much more comprehensive code, having 272 rules compared with 174 in the original edition. This is no reflection on the previous code, rather does it reflect the imposing development of libraries and their contents in the intervening years.

A detailed knowledge of the AACR may not be essential at this stage of the aspirant librarian's studies, but an early opportunity should be taken to examine the volume. It will be seen that the code is separated into three parts, one devoted to Entry and Heading, the second to Description, and the third to Nonbook materials. Within these parts are chapters given over to such topics as Headings for persons, Headings for corporate bodies, Uniform titles, Photographic and other reproductions, Manuscripts, Maps, Motion pictures and filmstrips, Phonorecords and Pictures.

The Rules are given clearly and succinctly, but notable features are the copious examples which should help practising cataloguers immensely in application. Attention is also drawn to the six appendices, the first of which is a glossary of cataloguing and bibliographical terms of prime importance to all students. The second appendix covers Capitalization, and guides the cataloguer as to when and when not to use capital letters. In the aim for consistency in catalogues this is a difficult enough problem in the English language, but this helpful appendix not only offers guidance here, but also has rules for capitalization in many foreign languages which may be unfamiliar to the cataloguer. Among these are Czech, Finnish, Russian and the Scandinavian languages.

A third appendix is devoted to abbreviations to be used in catalogue entries, and here again these are provided in Greek, Cyrillic and Hebraic alphabets as well as in a variety of foreign languages. Other appendices cover numerals and punctuation, while the sixth and final appendix is of particular interest because it isolates those rules for entry and heading that are different in the North American text. The volume is completed by a comprehensive index with references to rule numbers.

It behoves every student to examine this volume with great care in order to appreciate its contents. More detailed study of the individual rules can follow at a later stage. While the 1967 edition of the British text of the AACR may be regarded as definitive, nothing is ever final, and a revised edition is being prepared. But the revisers have a fine definitive text to use as a base.

DESCRIPTION

As already noted, the fullest form of entry in a catalogue is reserved for the main entry, that is the author entry in a dictionary catalogue, and the entry under subject in a classified catalogue. There are, in fact, so many details to be included that rules exist to ensure a uniform order for them. The details are known as the *description* and a possible order for them is as follows:

Author's name
Title (in the form given on the book's title-page)
Edition (after first)

IMPRINT
Place of publication
Name of publisher
Date of publication
Standard book number

COLLATION
Number of volumes and/or pages
Illustrations (type of illus. in following order)
    frontispiece (*frontis.* or *front.*)
    illustrations (*illus.*)
    plates (*pls.*)
    photos (*photos*)
    portraits (*portrs.*)
    maps (*maps*)
    plans (*plans*)
    facsimiles (*facsims.*)
    tables (*tabs.*)
    diagrams (*diagrs.*)
Size (height in cms.)
Series note (where applicable)
Contents (if necessary)
Annotation (if necessary)

Few books will require a description containing all the above items, but they would still be necessary if one were preparing, say, a catalogue of a small specialized collection designed to be printed and published. It is worth noting that although a catalogue produced by computer programming has many advantages, it has some drawbacks too, one of which is that many computers limit the number of characters to be reproduced, and full detailed entries are not always possible. Before concluding this section, it should also be mentioned that some title-pages, particularly those of older books from the seventeenth and eighteenth centuries, are very wordy and it is not always necessary to transcribe them word for word. Much is left to the discretion of the cataloguer, but if he does omit anything he should indicate the omission by the customary three dots . . . a legitimate device for noting that something has been left out.

CO-OPERATIVE OR CENTRAL CATALOGUING

Librarians have been concerned for many years with the question of co-operative or central cataloguing. As the term suggests, this name is applied to attempts to catalogue books from a central agency, leaving libraries to purchase their requirements and saving them the time, trouble and expense of cataloguing the books themselves. In the United States the Library of Congress has long been responsible for the central cataloguing of books and the distribution of printed catalogue cards to subscribing libraries. In the Scandinavian countries this kind of service is provided by the various library supply agencies, such as the Bibliotekstjänst at Lund in Sweden, and Bibliotekscentralen at Copenhagen. Similar services are available to libraries in Holland, West Germany, Romania and numerous other countries.

In the United Kingdom, when the *British National Bibliography* began publication in 1950 many librarians were disappointed that its services did not include printed entries on cards or slips, but time soon remedied this state of affairs and for a number of years now BNB has provided this service. For one reason or another, however, British libraries have not given this service the support it perhaps deserved. Another central cataloguing service is that provided by Her Majesty's Stationery Office which issues, on a subscription basis, printed catalogue cards for all Government publications.

The advent of the computer has brought a new dimension to this problem. To assist the growing number of libraries which now use and rely upon computers, the Library of Congress has in recent years been producing what are known as MARC tapes. The initials stand for Machine Readable Cataloguing. To its credit, BNB was quick to realize the possibilities and, collaborating with the Library of Congress, it also is now producing BNB/MARC tapes for use in libraries generally. This admirable project was supported by funds from the Office for Scientific and Technical Information (OSTI).

A revolution in cataloguing has therefore begun. With the gradual elimination of smaller library units, the larger library systems will have more possibilities of utilizing computers and either producing their own magnetic tapes or else making use of the BNB/MARC Project. Now that BNB has become part of the British Library we may expect many further developments.

Chapter 10
Bibliographies and reference material

A knowledge in depth of bibliographies and reference material is a basic essential for all librarians, in whatever type of library they are working. Numerous books are available on the subject approach to books, an example being Ronald Staveley's *Notes on Subject Bibliography*, and on reference material, of which a good recent example is the ALA publication *Fundamental Reference Sources*, by Frances Neel Cheney. At a later stage, student librarians will need detailed recourse to these and other books, but they should become familiar with them even now, at the primary stage of their studies. There are, in addition, several excellent annotated guides to reference sources, among them being A. J. Walford's *Guide to Reference Material*, a British publication which is paralleled by the American *Guide to Reference Books*, by Constance M. Winchell.

In amassing experience in the knowledge and use of reference materials and bibliographies there is no real alternative to constant practical experience in the use of them. However, the student librarian is fortunate indeed if he can gain this experience and practical knowledge in a good reference library in his early days. If, as most are, he is deprived of this practical experience he must instead obtain acquaintance with such material by personal handling, and by making notes on the arrangement, contents and scope of well-known bibliographies and reference books.

On the other hand, if he can get actual working experience in a department of a library which is handling reference and information work, so much the better. He will soon discover that such work resembles literary detection. Many and varied enquiries come thick and fast from readers, and only by personal knowledge of the range and contents of a wide range of reference material can these posers be readily answered. If actual experience cannot be obtained, visits to and personal use of other good reference libraries are recommended. Textbooks and lectures on reference and information work can help by pointing the way, but real intimacy with the material can be achieved only by the student himself exploring the avenues.

BIBLIOGRAPHIES

One of the basic disciplines which is required study by all librarians is a knowledge of bibliographies, of which there are an alarming number. Only the most salient ones will be mentioned here, but it is hoped that the student may be led on to acquaint himself with many more. Bibliographies may be international, national, subject or author, but in addition to these there are numerous bibliographies of bibliographies. Among these must be mentioned such works as Theodore Besterman's *A World Bibliography of Bibliographies*, which was first published in two volumes in 1939-40, and is now in its fourth edition, issued in 1965-66. Attention is also drawn to *Bibliographic Index: A Cumulative Bibliography of Bibliographies*, published twice-yearly in New York by the H. W. Wilson Co. and cumulated annually and three-yearly. R. L. Collison's *Bibliographies: Subject and National* should also be inspected. This was first issued in 1951 and is at present in its third edition, 1968.

Many countries now issue national bibliographies. For the United Kingdom the current national bibliography is BNB which has already been described earlier in this book, but there are numerous retrospective bibliographies of British literature. Among these must be cited Pollard and Redgrave's *Short-title Catalogue* which lists books printed in England, Scotland and Ireland, and English books printed abroad in the years 1475 to 1640. This is continued by Wing's *Short-title Catalogue* which covers the years 1641 to 1700. Other essential contributions to the national bibliography of Britain will be found in the *English Catalogue of Books*, which has been running since 1801; Whitaker's *Cumulative Book List*, which has appeared since 1924 in quarterly, annual and quinquennial cumulations; *British Books in Print*, which has appeared since 1965 but was previously known as *The Reference Catalogue of Current Literature*; and *Paperbacks in Print*, which began under another title in 1960.

Basic information about European books may be found in the national bibliographies which are produced in almost every country. Good examples are *Svensk Bokförteckning* (Sweden), *Bibliographie de Belgique* (Belgium), and the national bibliographies of such countries as Germany, the USSR and Romania. In the Commonwealth, Australia began a national bibliography in 1961, and New Zealand in 1967, though in each case these were continuations of earlier publications.

As one would expect, the United States is well covered bibliographically. The work with which all student librarians should acquaint themselves is the *Cumulative Book Index*, or CBI, which has appeared since 1898. It appears monthly and is cumulated at longer intervals, especially annually. An important point to note about CBI is that it lists not only books in the English language published in the USA, but many of those published abroad as well. Students should also be familiar with *Books in Print*, which appears annually in two volumes, the first being author-arranged, and the second listing is by titles. This is described by Walford as 'an invaluable finding-list of c. 250,000 titles available from 1,600 US publishers'.

In addition to the national bibliographies, and it must be stressed that only a few of these have been mentioned above, librarians need to be aware of the value of many printed library catalogues. The British Museum's *General Catalogue of Printed Books* has already been mentioned in an earlier chapter, but it must not be forgotten in this context. Other library catalogues of note are those of the London Library, the Bibliothèque Nationale in Paris, the University of California, and the Library of Congress. The latter also produces the *National Union Catalog*, which is an absolutely essential tool for tracing American books.

Mention should also be made of some reference books which give information on book auction prices. British examples of these are *Book-Auction Records* and *Book-prices Current*, while American examples are *American Book-prices Current*, and *Bookman's Price Index*.

The field of periodicals is one which does not easily lend itself to bibliographical control, but a great deal of information about them is nevertheless available both on an international and a national basis. The *British Union Catalogue of Periodicals*, sometimes known as BUCOP, was issued between 1955 and 1958 in four volumes, and from 1964 it has been continued by the National Central Library quarterly with annual cumulations. Another important guide, this time American, is Ulrich's *International Periodicals Directory*, first issued in 1932. By 1970 this had reached its 13th edition, and was listing over 40,000 periodicals, mainly American but offering increasing coverage of the journals issued in countries outside the United States.

Indexes to periodicals are necessary components of bibliographical coverage. The Library Association itself has made important contributions in this field, notably *British Humanities Index* and *British Technology Index*. The former dates back to 1915, being originally issued under the title of *Subject Index to Periodicals*, but its name was changed to *British Humanities Index* in 1962. It now appears quarterly, and is cumulated into an annual volume. *British Technology Index*, or BTI, was first issued in 1962: it appears monthly and like BHI it is also cumulated annually. Other countries also have their indexes to periodicals, notably the *Readers' Guide to Periodical Literature*, published by the H. W. Wilson Co. of New York since 1905, *Dansk Tidsskrift-index*, issued in Copenhagen since 1915, and the *Canadian Index to Periodicals and Documentary Films*, published by the Canadian Library Association since 1949.

Not only periodicals but also important newspapers are indexed, and the results published in book form. Among the newspapers so indexed are *The Times*, the *New York Times*, the *Glasgow Herald* and *Le Monde*. In some countries selective indexing is done of the more important articles in newspapers, notable examples being *Avis-kronik-index* (Danish), the *Indian News Index*, and the *Canadian News Index*.

Student librarians must also make themselves aware of the existence of abstracts, of which a great number are now published. In our own field there is *Library and Information Science Abstracts* (LISA), published by the Library Association since 1950, though from that year until 1969 this was issued under the title of *Library Science Abstracts* (LSA). In America there is issued *Library Literature*, though this is an index rather than an abstracting service. In other fields there are many examples, such as *Chemical Abstracts*, *Engineering Abstracts* and *Fuel Abstracts*.

Earlier mention was made of the fact that there are many bibliographies in existence relating to specific subjects and individual authors. So as not to confuse the student with too many titles, one or two examples only are quoted. As a subject bibliography, the *Cambridge Bibliography of English Literature* is mentioned, while a distinguished bibliography of an author is Sir Geoffrey Keynes' *Bibliography of William Blake*. It should also be mentioned that there are examples of bibliographies of special classes of writers, such as Halkett and Laing's *Dictionary of Anonymous and Pseudonymous Literature*.

REFERENCE BOOKS

Turning now to reference books generally, we find many types including encyclopaedias, annuals, dictionaries, directories, gazetteers, atlases and biographical dictionaries, and all these may be general or specific.

General encyclopaedias include the *Encyclopaedia Britannica*, *Chambers's Encyclopaedia*, the *Encyclopedia Americana*, and *Collier's Encyclopedia*, while a good instance of a specific encyclopaedia is *Grove's Dictionary of Music and Musicians*. General annuals include the well-known *Whitaker's Almanack* and the *World Almanac and Book of Facts*, the latter being the American counterpart of the British *Whitaker*. Later references will be made to some other well-known annuals.

Dictionaries of etymology are led by the *Oxford English Dictionary*, which is in twelve volumes and a supplement. It is sometimes known as the *New English Dictionary*, or Murray, after the name of its first editor. It should not be forgotten that there are other versions, such as the *Shorter Oxford English Dictionary*, the *Concise Oxford English Dictionary*, and the *Oxford Illustrated English Dictionary*. Among shorter dictionaries of British origin may be mentioned *Chambers's Twentieth Century Dictionary*, a new edition of which appeared in 1972. From America, *Webster's Third New International Dictionary* is deservedly celebrated, as is the *Random House Dictionary of the English Language*.

Most countries have standard monolingual dictionaries of their own languages, and there are especially good examples in France (Larousse) and the Scandinavian countries (Gyldendals).

Examples of bilingual dictionaries abound, but perhaps the classic example is that of a classic language. This is the work by

Liddell and Scott entitled *A Greek–English Lexicon*. A more modern instance is *Harrap's Standard French and English Dictionary*, edited by J. E. Mansion, which Walford describes as falling 'little short of lexicographical perfection as a bilingual dictionary'.

Then there are dictionaries of specific subjects, but it has to be remarked that often these are encyclopaedias rather than dictionaries. However, an example may be quoted from our own discipline in the shape of Harrod's *Librarians' Glossary*, which is a dictionary of terms used in librarianship and the book crafts.

Directories are published in many forms, and they are among the most used of quick-reference books. In Britain the Post Office telephone directories are regularly issued for different areas, and classified (trades and professional) directories are also available. Foreign telephone directories, such as those for Ireland, France, Holland and the United States, are available on a subscription basis from the Post Office. The largest reference libraries find it necessary to stock telephone directories from all over the world. They are used as often for providing addresses as they are for providing telephone numbers, and are invaluable to those engaged in exporting and in commercial correspondence. In addition, many commercial directories are issued, such as *Kelly's Directory of Merchants, Manufacturers and Shippers*, also street directories such as the *Post Office London Directory* or Kelly's directories of most of the large cities and towns of the United Kingdom.

Time-tables are a source of information which student librarians must utilize and master as soon as possible, especially as most enquirers seem unable to use them properly, or profess to be unable to do so. As well as the *ABC Railway Guide*, those published by British Railways themselves should be known and used. Continental railway time-tables are in increasing demand, so *Cook's Continental Timetable* should be studied. For buses and coaches the *ABC Coach and Bus Guide* gives details of regular services in Great Britain and on the Continent, while for air journeys the *ABC World Airways Guide* is essential. All these publications contain prefatory directions as to their use, and these should be carefully studied as they undoubtedly save the time of the user.

Atlases and gazetteers will surely be represented in all libraries by *The Times Atlas of the World* and the *Columbia Lippincott Gazetteer of the World*. The former originally appeared in parts from 1920 to 1922 but from 1955 to 1960 a new edition, the Mid-century edition, appeared in five volumes. The whole atlas presents cartography par excellence, the maps being based on the latest surveys and exploration. Each volume is self-contained with its own index. A gazetteer is an alphabetical list of places, rivers, lakes, mountains and other geographical features giving information as to their whereabouts. Certainly the best world gazetteer is the *Columbia Lippincott Gazetteer of the World* which, in addition to providing all the required information about world geographical features, however small or remote, offers helpful advice on the pronunciation of place-names, and gives the populations of cities, towns, villages and hamlets. *Webster's Geographical Dictionary* is a smaller though still monumental work, while for the British Isles Bartholomew's have published a useful gazetteer.

Bartholomew's have also produced a good range of smaller atlases, as well as the celebrated *Reference Atlas of Greater London*. Sheet maps of different countries of the world will be stocked by the best reference libraries, and for the United Kingdom the Ordnance Survey maps are the most reliable. Road maps are of great importance these days, and some of the best examples are those produced by the Rand McNally Company in the United States.

Biographical information is frequently called for by users of reference libraries, but fortunately there are many biographical dictionaries available. These may be retrospective, such as the *Dictionary of National Biography* (for Britain) or the *Dictionary of American Biography* (for the United States). These are multi-volume works of a standard nature, but there are one-volume retrospective biographical dictionaries such as those published by Chambers's and Webster's. Current biographical dictionaries include *Who's Who*, *Who's Who in America*, the *International Who's Who*, and indeed a large number of reference books giving current biographical information for individual countries such as Germany, Italy, Finland and so on. It is important to remember that a work like *Who's Who* is supplemented by retrospective volumes entitled *Who Was Who*, which has now reached its sixth volume. This is paralleled in the United States by *Who Was Who in America*.

Just as happens in the case of other reference books, biographical dictionaries cover specific fields as well as the general. British examples of these are *Who's Who in the Theatre*, *The Authors' and Writers' Who's Who*, and *Who's Who in Librarianship and Information Science*, while in the United States there are such titles as *Contemporary Authors*, *American Men of Science*, *Who's Who in Commerce and Industry*, and *A Biographical Dictionary of Librarians in the United States and Canada*. The latter was formerly entitled *Who's Who in Library Service*.

From the plethora of other reference material available, a few more general and well-known titles must be isolated, since they are stocked in the smallest reference libraries and aspirant librarians must acquaint themselves with their scope. One of these is *Brewer's Dictionary of Phrase and Fable*. How better can one describe this unique reference book than by citing its subtitle – 'the derivation, source or origin of common phrases, allusions and words that have a tale to tell'. One might also quote a phrase of the compiler's when he described his book as 'a treasury of literary bric-a-brac'. It is, in fact, a monumental compilation of words and phrases, alphabetically arranged, with explanations. Dr Brewer also compiled a *Readers' Handbook*, dealing specifically with literary allusions, references, proverbs, plots and characters.

While on the topic of literary characters it should be remembered that there exist a large number of reference books relating to characters in fiction. A general example is Freeman's *Dictionary of Fictional Characters*, supplemented by author and title indexes prepared by J. M. F. Leaper. As applied to individual authors there are published dictionaries relating to the characters in the works of Jane Austen, George Eliot, Hardy and Kipling, to quote but a few.

Books of quotations are in frequent demand. *The Oxford Dictionary of Quotations* is a standard work, but other useful compilations are *Bartlett's Familiar Quotations* and *Stevenson's Home Book of Quotations*. Once again, this technique is manifested in a more specialized way, so that we have *Stevenson's Book of Shakespeare Quotations*, and the *Oxford Dictionary of English Proverbs*.

Mention of the Oxford University Press draws attention to the numerous other examples of reference books from this source. These include the *Oxford Companion to English Literature*, the *Oxford Companion to American Literature*, the *Oxford Companion to Music*, and similar compendia on art, the theatre, classical literature, American history, French literature, and Canadian history and literature. These are encylopaedic in form and offer outline and reliable information.

This chapter is concluded with details of just a few of the many standard and serial publications of a reference character with which all student librarians should make themselves familiar. In the field of religion there is *Cruden's Concordance to the Old and New Testaments* which was first published in 1737 and has since been re-issued many times by different publishers. It comprises phrases and quotations from the Bible, and refers the enquirer to chapters and verses. Undoubtedly, Cruden is a vast store-house of information on the Bible, its contents and its allusions.

The official reference book of the Church of England is *Crockford's Clerical Directory* and it has been so since it first appeared in 1858. Until 1948 it appeared annually, but since then it has appeared less regularly. It contains a who's who of the Church of England clergy, as well as general information on the Church, its cathedrals, archbishops, bishops and establishments. In every issue of Crockford there is a preface which is usually very topical and invariably controversial. Most other churches have their regular publications, and among these are the *Catholic Directory*, the *Congregational Year-book*, the *Baptist Handbook*, and the *Church of Scotland Year-book*. A most useful general reference book of Christianity is the *Oxford Dictionary of the Christian Church*, first issued in 1957 and prepared on the same lines as the Oxford companions described above.

Historical reference books include Haydn's *Dictionary of Dates* which first appeared in 1841 and has had many editions since then. A similar work is *Newnes' Dictionary of Dates*, by R. L. Collison, first published in 1962. Both these give ready-reference facts on the dating of events in history, as well as including historical characters. For the British nobility the essential work of reference is *Debrett's Peerage, Baronetage,*

Knightage and Companionage, an annual compendium containing a great deal of information on the Royal Family, the nobility and on governmental, diplomatic and consular circles. Full biographical details are provided for peers, baronets, knights and their families, and also for companions of orders.

Among the many year books which are issued regularly are the *Statesman's Year Book*, the *Municipal Year Book*, *Kempe's Engineer's Year Book*, the *Writers' and Artists' Year Book*, and *Willing's Press Guide*. The *Statesman's Year Book* has appeared annually since 1864. It is a reference book about the countries of the world containing statistics and general information about them. It has also good sections about the United Nations, its membership, organs, budgets and specialized agencies such as UNESCO and UNRRA.

The *Municipal Year Book and Public Utilities Directory*, to give it its full title, is the standard reference book for local government in the United Kingdom and the Republic of Ireland. It reviews the previous year's work and then lists all local authorities, giving information on their populations, areas, finances, members of councils and names of chief and senior officers. Full statistical tables are provided for each local government activity, such as housing, education, health, libraries and so on. *Kempe's Engineer's Year Book* has appeared annually since 1894. It contains data, formulae, tables and memoranda of use to civil, mechanical, electrical, marine, gas, steam, oil, metallurgical and mining engineers. It is best approached via its excellent relative index, and it also contains a useful buyers' guide, a classified directory of leading engineering and allied firms.

The *Writers' and Artists' Year Book* is an annual which first appeared in 1908. Beginning with a journalist's calendar, which is useful for giving centenaries and anniversaries, the main section follows and is an alphabetical list of British journals and magazines, giving the names of their editors, addresses, descriptions of their contents, their requirements in the way of literary and artistic material, and their rates of payment. Similar directories, though necessarily briefer, are given for Commonwealth and American journals. A reference section offers useful articles on copyright, libel, censorship, performing rights, proof correcting and other topics of interest to writers and artists. Of special interest to librarians are the list of pen-names and pseudonyms, and the classified index of journals and magazines, in which periodicals are arranged according to the subjects they cover.

Another standard reference book is *Willing's Press Guide*, which has been published annually since 1871. This is mainly an alphabetical list of newspapers and periodicals published in the United Kingdom and the Republic of Ireland, giving the year of establishment of the publication, its frequency, price and the address of its editorial offices. Following this is a classified list, after which the *Press Guide* goes on to list dominion, colonial and foreign publications. Much other useful information is contained in the book including, among other items, the London addresses of provincial publications, details of film and TV newsreels, and a list of reporting and news agencies.

Professional registers are useful and much-used reference material, and these include such publications as the *Law List*, the *Medical Register*, the *Dentists' Register* and the *Library Association Year Book*.

Finally a miscellany of standard reference books which must of necessity be handled by every aspirant librarian. These include the *Annual Register of World Events*, Fox-Davies's *Armorial Families*, Beaumont's *Complete Book of Ballets*, Mrs Beeton's *Book of Household Management*, Black's *Medical Dictionary*, Burke's *Peerage, Baronetage and Knightage*, *Every Man's Own Lawyer*, Fowler's *Modern English Usage*, the *Guinness Book of Records*, Jane's *All the World's Aircraft*, the *McGraw-Hill Encyclopedia of Science and Technology*, *Roget's Thesaurus of English Words and Phrases*, and such standards as Chaffers on English porcelain, and Edwards on English furniture. One could go on almost ad infinitum, but an end must be called. Readers may wish to amuse themselves by joining the critics who will search for omissions. Meanwhile, the student may wish to be referred to the present author's book *Facts at Your Fingertips*, a guide to reference books which was written for the man in the street but which apparently has also been found useful to those studying librarianship.

Suggested further reading

Place of publication is London unless otherwise stated.

ADAMS, W. G. S. *Report on Library Provision and Policy.* CUKT. Dunfermline, 1915.

ASHWORTH, WILFRED. *Handbook of Special Librarianship.* 3rd ed. Aslib. 1967.

BATTY, C. D. *An Introduction to the Eighteenth Edition of the Dewey Decimal Classification.* Clive Bingley. 1971.

BURRELL, T. W. *Learn To Use Books and Libraries.* Clive Bingley. 1969.

CHENEY, FRANCES NEEL. *Fundamental Reference Sources.* ALA. Chicago, 1971.

CORBETT, E. V. *An Introduction to Librarianship.* 2nd ed. James Clarke. 1970 reprint.

CURRALL, H. F. J. (*ed.*). *Gramophone Record Libraries.* 2nd ed. Crosby, Lockwood. 1970.

FOSKETT, D. J. *Information Service in Libraries.* 2nd ed. Crosby, Lockwood. 1967.

GREAT BRITAIN. *Report of the Departmental Committee on Public Libraries* (Kenyon Report). HMSO. 1927.

GREAT BRITAIN (Ministry of Education). *The Structure of the Public Library Service in England and Wales* (Roberts Report). HMSO. 1959.

GREAT BRITAIN (Department of Education and Science). *Report of the National Libraries Committee* (Dainton Report). HMSO. 1969.

HARRISON, K. C. *Facts at Your Fingertips: Everyman's Guide to Reference Books.* 2nd ed. Kenneth Mason. Havant, 1966.

HARRISON, K. C. *Libraries in Britain.* Longmans for the British Council. 1968.

HEEKS, PEGGY. *Administration of Children's Libraries.* Library Association. 1967. (LA Pamphlet no. 30.)

HORNER, JOHN. *Cataloguing.* AAL. 1970.

HARROD, L. M. *The Librarians' Glossary.* 3rd ed. André Deutsch. 1971.

LEWIS, M. JOY. *Libraries for the Handicapped.* Library Association. 1969. (LA Pamphlet no. 33.)

LIBRARY ASSOCIATION. *Anglo-American Cataloguing Rules. British Text.* Library Association. 1967.

11

LIBRARY ASSOCIATION. *School Library Resource Centres.* Library Association. 1970.

LIBRARY ASSOCIATION. *Students' Handbook.* Library Association. Annual.

LIBRARY ASSOCIATION. *Year Book.* Library Association. Annual.

MUNFORD, W. A. (*ed.*). *Annals of the Library Association, 1877 to 1960.* Library Association. 1965.

STOCKHAM, K. A. (*ed.*). *British County Libraries, 1919–1969.* André Deutsch. 1969.

STOCKHAM, K. A. *The Government and Control of Libraries.* André Deutsch. 1968.

THOMPSON, G. A. (*ed.*). *The Technical College Library: A Primer for Its Development.* André Deutsch. 1968.

UNIVERSITY GRANTS COMMITTEE. *Report of the Committee on Libraries* (Parry Report). HMSO. 1967.

WALFORD, A. J. (*ed.*). *Guide to Reference Material.* 3 vols. Library Association. 1966–70.

WHITAKER, KENNETH. *Using Libraries.* 3rd ed. André Deutsch. 1972.

WOODWORTH, DAVID (*ed.*). *Guide to Current British Journals.* Library Association. 1971.

Appendix
List of Abbreviations

AAL	Association of Assistant Librarians
ABLS	Association of British Library Schools
ACGB	Arts Council of Great Britain
ALA	Associate of the Library Association; American Library Association
ALCL	Association of London Chief Librarians
AMC	Association of Municipal Corporations
APLET	Association for Programmed Learning and Educational Technology
Aslib	Association of Special Libraries and Information Bureaux
ATCDE	Association of Teachers in Colleges and Departments of Education
BA	Booksellers' Association
BCM	*British Catalogue of Music*
BEI	*British Education Index*
BHI	*British Humanities Index*
BL	British Library
BML	British Museum Library
BNB	*British National Bibliography*
BNBC	British National Book Centre
BSI	British Standards Institution
BTI	*British Technology Index*
BUCOP	*British Union Catalogue of Periodicals*
CBI	Cumulative Book Index
CCA	County Councils Association
CICRIS	Co-operative, Industrial and Commercial Reference and Information Service
CML	Central Music Library
CNAA	Council for National Academic Awards
COCRIL	Council of City Research and Information Libraries
COM	Computer Output Microfilm
COMLA	Commonwealth Library Association
CRG	Classification Research Group
CUKT	Carnegie United Kingdom Trust

DC	Decimal Classification (Dewey)
DES	Department of Education and Science
DSIR	Department of Scientific and Industrial Research
EKZ	Einkaufzentrale für öffentliche Büchereien
FID	Fédération Internationale de Documentation
FLA	Fellow of the Library Association
HMSO	Her Majesty's Stationery Office
HERTIS	Hertfordshire Technical Information Service
HULTIS	Hull Technical Information Service
IAML	International Association of Music Libraries
IATUL	International Association of Technological University Libraries
IFLA	International Federation of Library Associations
INTAMEL	International Association of Metropolitan City Libraries
JFR	Joint Fiction Reserve
LA	Library Association
LADSIRLAC	Liverpool and District Scientific, Industrial and Research Library Advisory Council
LAR	*Library Association Record*
LASER	London and South Eastern Library Region
LC	Library of Congress; Local Collection
LETIS	Leicester and Leicestershire Technical Information Service
LISA	*Library and Information Science Abstracts*
LSA	*Library Science Abstracts*
LUC	London Union Catalogue
LULOP	*London Union List of Periodicals*
MARC	Machine readable cataloguing
MEDLARS	Medical Literature Analysts and Retrieval System
MJFR	Metropolitan Joint Fiction Reserve
MS or MSS	Manuscript or Manuscripts
MSC	Metropolitan Special Collections
NALGO	National Association of Local and Government Officers
NANTIS	Nottingham and Nottinghamshire Technical Information Service
NBL	National Book League
NCAVAE	National Committee for Audio-Visual Aids in Education
NCET	National Council for Educational Technology
NCL	National Central Library
NCRLC	National Committee for Regional Library Co-operation
ND	No date
NLA	National Libraries Authority

NLB	National Library for the Blind
NLLST (NLL)	National Lending Library for Science and Technology
NRLSI	National Reference Library of Science and Invention
OED	*Oxford English Dictionary*
OP	Out-of-print
OSTI	Office for Scientific and Technical Information
PA	Publishers' Association
PPBS	Programme Planned Budgeting Systems
RLS	Regional Library System
SCL	Scottish Central Library
SCOLLUL	Standing Conference of Librarians of the Libraries of the University of London
SCOLMA	Standing Conference on Library Materials on Africa
SCONUL	Standing Conference on National and University Libraries
SCOTAPLL	Standing Conference of Theological and Philosophical Libraries in London
SINTO	Sheffield Interchange Organization
SLA	Scottish Library Association; School Library Association
SMCCL	Society of Municipal and County Chief Librarians
SS	Subject specialization
TALIC	Tyneside Association of Libraries for Industry and Commerce
UDC	Universal Decimal Classification; Urban District Council
UGC	University Grants Committee
UNESCO	United Nations Educational, Scientific and Cultural Organisation
WEA	Workers' Educational Association
WLA	Welsh Library Association

Index

Index